DISCOVERING YOUR
PAST LIVES

Made Easy

❖ **Also in the Made Easy series** ❖

DISCOVERING YOUR
PAST LIVES

Made Easy

Connect with Your Past Lives to
Create Positive Change

ATASHA FYFE

HAY HOUSE

Carlsbad, California • New York City
London • Sydney • New Delhi

Published in the United Kingdom by:
Hay House UK, Ltd.,The Sixth Floor, Watson House, 54 Baker Street, London
W1U 7BU • Phone: +44 (0)20 3927 7290 • Fax: +44 (0)20 3927 7291
www.hayhouse.co.uk

Published in the United States of America by:
Hay House Inc., PO Box 5100, Carlsbad, CA 92018-5100
Tel: (1) 760 431 7695 or (800) 654 5126
Fax: (1) 760 431 6948 or (800) 650 5115; www.hayhouse.com

Published in Australia by:
Hay House Australia Ltd, 18/36 Ralph St, Alexandria NSW 2015
Tel: (61) 2 9669 4299; Fax: (61) 2 9669 4144; www.hayhouse.com.au

Published in India by:
Hay House Publishers India, Muskaan Complex, Plot No.3, B-2,
Vasant Kunj, New Delhi 110 070
Tel: (91) 11 4176 1620; Fax: (91) 11 4176 1630; www.hayhouse.co.in

This book was previously published under the title *Past Lives* (*Hay House
Basics* series); ISBN: 978-1-78180-265-6

A catalogue record for this book is available from the British Library.

ISBN: 978-1-4019-7785-6
Ebook ISBN: 978-1-78817-253-0

Interior images: Bruce Rolff /123RF

Printed in the United States of America

This product uses papers sourced from responsibly managed forests. For more
information, see www.hayhouse.com.

*'I hold that when a person dies
His soul returns again to Earth;
Arrayed in some new flesh-disguise
Another mother gives him birth.'*

JOHN MASEFIELD

Contents

List of Exercises

Introduction

Your past lives are not dead and gone. They are a living part of your greater identity. Just knowing this can change your life. You see reality in a new, expanded way; you no longer fear death; and you understand so much more about your self, your relationships and your current life.

Even before you know about them, your past lives are a strong influence in your life. This influence is usually positive – but sometimes it can also be negative. The golden key that heals those bad effects is finding out about the past life when the problem began. Past-life therapy has shown beyond doubt that this can resolve an amazingly wide range of issues.

As you get to know about your past lives, you'll also be bringing in all their positive effects. Your past selves have great gifts for you – the many prizes you won through experiences and tests that you passed along your soul path. It's invaluable to know about this positive side of your history as well. So how do you start?

There's an old saying: 'When the student is ready, the teacher appears'. I've found this to be just as true about remembering past lives. When we're ready to meet them, they step forward and start to introduce themselves. Not all at once, of course – that would be too much to handle.

It's a gentle process that happens little by little, like a flower opening up one petal at a time. The seed of that flower may have been planted much earlier, staying dormant for years until conditions were right for it to grow.

For example, one of my regression clients told me that the first time she ever heard about past lives was in a magazine story. It was a tale about how an old love had returned from a previous life. She said she'd enjoyed the story, but didn't delve any deeper into the idea of reincarnation.

It was only many years later that she began to wonder about her own former lives. Issues with her partner were bothering her, so she came for a regression. She discovered that their problem really had come from a previous lifetime together. With that knowledge, she was able to sort things out. The seed planted by the magazine love story had grown and flowered at just the right time for her.

The first time I heard about past lives was from my Scottish father. He wasn't at all religious or mystical – but was convinced that he'd had a past life in America. On looking back I think he was probably right. It would explain why he was always reading books about the Wild West, and why his favourite magazines were the *Saturday Evening Post* and *The New Yorker*.

Sometimes he made passing remarks about his past-life theory. He might as well have said it was chilly for the time of year for all the attention it ever got. But although we never discussed it, we also never opposed the idea.

I think now that this must have been when the seed of past-life awareness was first planted in my childhood. Of course, I had no idea what strange flowers that seed would later produce.

The first sign I had of the past-life drama that lay in wait for me was at the age of 17. I had a vivid dream that I've never forgotten. It was during the French Revolution. I was about to be guillotined. When I put my head on the chopping block, I was shocked to feel the wet blood of previous victims on my throat. At that point the dream suddenly ended, and I woke up with a gasp.

Since then I've had many more dreams about the French Revolution. I've also found out about the past life I had at that time. I wasn't an aristocrat, but was part of the new middle class. As an idealistic young man, I believed in the revolution and tried to promote its ideals.

But in the end, like so many others, I was arrested, given a show trial, and sent on my way to the next world. After that experience, I decided that I would never again speak out openly about what I believed in. It was far too dangerous.

That fear created an unconscious block in my psyche that then held me back like invisible chains. Becoming aware of that, and dealing with it, was a major part of my journey towards writing about past lives. If I hadn't understood that problem and where it came from, this book would never have been written.

This is how dramatically past-life awareness can change our lives. Although I've summed it up in a few short paragraphs, this process took a while. These important changes are too big to happen overnight. So there's no need to push the river. Your past life plant will grow in its own way and its own time. The fact that you're reading this now is a sign that it's already flowering for you.

You also don't need to remember every single past life you ever had. Even if you only find out about one or two, you'll automatically receive the great gifts that past-life awareness has for us.

Those gifts are the many ways in which your life will become enriched. Simply knowing that you had past lives creates a happier, more meaningful and more fulfilled experience of life in the present.

An expanding new consciousness is now taking place in the world. I'm convinced that past-life awareness is an important part of that. It brings personal and spiritual benefits for everyone. It has the power to change our lives. It fosters more tolerance and understanding of others. And it will ultimately transform the kind of world we live in.

Chapter 1

Who Believes in Reincarnation?

The answer to this question is that almost every culture in the world throughout recorded history has believed in reincarnation – with one big exception. In the Western world, belief in past lives turned into a forbidden treasure. For the last 1,500 years the people of Christendom have sought it, hidden it and even died for it.

During this time Westerners largely forgot that the benefits of past-life awareness were part of their natural birthright. For centuries, people in Europe suffered far more than they needed to because this knowledge was kept from them. Those who did believe in reincarnation were viciously persecuted.

As part of this control, the Church hid some key facts from the public. But in our modern age of literacy and freedom of information, we can now dig up that buried knowledge.

Some of the clues have always been there in plain sight. It's now obvious that the Bible is full of signs of belief in reincarnation. Writer Joe Fisher said 'Reincarnation teaching in the Bible is largely taken for granted, cropping up here and there as a fundamental rock.'

The Essenes, the Pharisees, the Nazarenes and the Egyptian Therapeutae all actively taught about reincarnation. In later centuries the early Christian Gnostics saw themselves as the direct continuation of the real teachings of Jesus – and reincarnation was central to Gnosticism.

It was also important to early Christianity. St Augustine and other renowned Church fathers both preached and wrote about reincarnation as a significant part of Christian faith.

How the Dark Ages really began

So what happened? One man alone was responsible for changing the nature of Christianity – and he wasn't even a member of the Church. It was the Emperor Justinian.

The stage for this was set when, in the early fourth century, Christianity became the official religion of the Roman Empire. From that time on it slowly and steadily turned into an instrument of state control. Heresy – which comes from the Greek word for 'choice' – was upgraded from being a belief that did not comply with established doctrines and was a mere sin to a serious crime that was punishable with death.

The widespread belief in reincarnation made it difficult for this new state-controlled Church to establish real authority. Knowing how rebirth works, people could take responsibility for their own salvation. They didn't need a priest to intervene for them. In their freedom, they were a direct threat to the Emperor's power base of orthodox Christianity.

The emperor's new law

So the Empire struck back. In AD529 Emperor Justinian closed the University of Athens, a major stronghold of reincarnation studies. The scholars fled for their lives. Many of them found refuge in Sufi centres further east. Then, in 553, Justinian made reincarnation a heresy. From that time on, anyone who said they believed in it would be executed.

Pope Virgilius and most of the Bishops were strongly against banning the belief in reincarnation. But the Emperor pushed it through anyway. He did this by calling a Council consisting only of the Bishops who would support him.

The Pope was potentially more of a problem. So Justinian had him arrested and put into prison. While there, the Pope desperately tried to issue a document protesting against the new rule, but it didn't work. The Emperor freed him only after he'd reluctantly signed his name to the anti-reincarnation orders. On his way home, the Pope died in Syracuse – probably murdered by Justinian's henchmen.

These events were the start of the true Dark Ages. The centuries that followed were stained by the blood and charred by the fires of the Holy Inquisition. Belief in rebirth had to go underground to survive.

During the Renaissance it popped back up for a while through the influence of Cosimo de Medici, Duke of Florence. But within a few years the Church had stamped it down again. Thoughts of past lives were once more erased from the people's minds.

For nearly 400 years after that, knowledge of reincarnation lived on only in the secret worlds of mystics and occultists such as cabalists, alchemists and the Rosicrucians.

The underground revolution

And there the matter quietly remained until the late nineteenth century. During that time, a new interest in spirituality began to blossom. Esoteric groups sprang up like mushrooms.

One of the most influential was the Theosophical Society, set up by Madame Blavatsky in New York in 1875. Theosophy brought Eastern thought to the West – and that included the concept of reincarnation.

Rudolf Steiner created the Anthroposophical Society in 1912. He said, 'Just as an age was once ready to receive the Copernican theory of the universe, so is our age ready for the ideas of reincarnation.'

In the decades that followed, this statement proved to be something of a prophecy.

The watershed: Bridey Murphy

In the first half of the twentieth century, belief in past lives was growing in the new spiritual underground. At that stage, however, people were still mostly unaware of it.

Then in 1956 Morey Bernstein published *The Search for Bridey Murphy*. This book burst reincarnation belief into the mainstream. It was about a woman who'd been regressed to a past life in Ireland in the eighteenth century. She recalled that life in great and specific detail.

A raging controversy blew up over it. Certain members of the Church and traditional psychologists were determined to invalidate the book. But when reporters went to Ireland to investigate, they found that many details from the regression were historically accurate.

As a result, Bernstein's book hit the bestseller charts. Reincarnation became the new craze. People gave 'come as you were' parties, drank 'past-life' cocktails and sang 'It seems that we have met before'.

How people created past-life therapy

By the 1950s, conventional psychology was happy about using regression. It was a good way of taking patients back to when their problem began. Of course, they were only meant to go back to an incident in their childhood. But to the discomfort of psychotherapists, clients would often go back to past lives to identify the origin of their issues.

In those days, if professional people said they took past lives seriously they'd lose their credibility, their reputation and probably their job as well. So they tended to keep quiet about it. But as the second half of the century unfolded, some brave pioneers began to buck the trend. They were the psychiatrists and psychologists who decided that their patients' problems really might have begun in a past life.

Many of them wrote ground-breaking books about how they discovered the importance of past-life memories. The public gave their resounding approval to these books – and past-life therapy was born.

Highly qualified people such as Professor Ian Stevenson embarked on thorough investigations into the whole subject. The evidence that these pioneers have produced is solid enough to prove both the reality of past lives and the validity of past-life regression.

New frontiers

The boundaries of past-life therapy are now expanding to include future lives, and memories of the between-life worlds. It's also become clear that during a regression we can get in direct touch with our higher guidance.

In the Western world, we've had to rediscover reincarnation completely. In some ways this is a good thing, because it means we can start afresh. Belief in rebirth may be as ancient as humankind, but this may be the first time in recorded history that reincarnation, regression and the value of past-life therapy have been so thoroughly investigated. As a result, there is now a growing awareness of past lives, and the many ways they can help us to understand ourselves, solve our problems and transform our lives.

The tale of how reincarnation belief was banned and then restored in the West is a dramatic one. It's a saga full of heroes, villains and other colourful characters. If you'd like to read about it in more detail, have a look at this article on my website: www.pastlivesglastonbury.co.uk/reincarnation-is-back.html

SUMMARY

- Reincarnation has always been an important part of religions all over the world. It was also an early Christian belief.

- In the sixth century, despite the opposition of the Church, Emperor Justinian made reincarnation a heresy. From then until modern times Christians who believed in it had to keep it secret or risk death.

- Over the last century, the Western world has been rediscovering reincarnation almost from scratch. Academics and professional people have done serious research on the subject and published influential books.

- These pioneers have validated not only reincarnation, but also past-life regression therapy.

Western belief in reincarnation has come out of the shadows at last. And it brings great gifts for us: the personal benefits of belief in rebirth; the healing power of past-life therapy; and, along with this greater understanding of ourselves and others, the potential for a more peaceful world.

Part I

HOW TO DISCOVER YOUR PAST LIVES

*'I did not begin when I was born.
I have been growing, developing,
through myriads of millenniums.'*
JACK LONDON

Introduction

Discovering your past lives is like finding that you live in a mansion, when you always thought you were confined to a tiny flat. You probably had inklings all along that there was something beyond the walls of that little flat. Then one magical day you found the door to the mansion. A whole new world opened up for you.

When you know that you've had past lives, every relationship, circumstance and event becomes easier to understand. Welcome light starts to shine not only on your path now, but on the way ahead as well.

There are two main ways to find out more about your past lives. One is by looking inward and the other is by looking outward.

The inner way

The best inner ways to get past-life information are:

- Regression

- Meditation

- Intuition

- Dreams

- Introspection – such as understanding the past-life causes of your likes and dislikes.

The outer way

Ancient philosophies have always said that the outer world reflects what's within us. It's like a mirror to our deeper selves. It shows us things about ourselves that we're not conscious of. This includes past-life information. So the outer way is about spotting the external clues to past lives that are around us all the time.

In *The Elixir and the Stone,* authors Baigent and Leigh said 'We are beginning to make vital and dynamic connections between our internal and external lives which would have been unthinkable some 35 to 40 years ago.'

The main ways our past lives show up in the outer world are:

- Relationships that are often the continuation of stories that have been unfolding for several lifetimes.

- Past-life talents, skills or abilities that seem to have come from nowhere.

- Past-life effects that our bodies carry, such as birth-marks, posture, mannerisms, weaknesses, strengths and health issues.

- Past-life mementoes in our lifestyle, décor, possessions and clothes.

- External triggers such as books, pictures, music, movies, tastes or smells, which can all help to wake up past-life memories.

- Visits to special places, such as a stone circle, a castle or an ancient temple, which may trigger vivid memories of past-life experiences there.

Part I of this book will go into detail about how to spot the past-life clues that are within and around you all the time. Once you know where to look, you'll see them everywhere. A new adventure of discovery will open up for you – without having to go beyond your own doorstep.

Chapter 2

How Regression Works

I love regression because it puts people directly in touch with their own inner wisdom. This makes it one of the most empowering of all the therapies.

Most people come for a regression about a current problem they feel might have originated in a former lifetime. Regression is effective because it can track the past-life cause of many things that are happening in our lives today.

It works because the subconscious mind is a huge store-house of information about all our lives and experiences. This information isn't passive – it's not like books in a library, which we can decide to read or ignore.

Although our past lives may be long gone, their memories remain alive within us. They play an active part in our psyche, continuing to influence us in all kinds of unconscious ways. This can have both beneficial and obstructive effects on our present life.

Past lives are like a fairy godmother that comes to us at birth. They endow us with all kinds of positive gifts, such as personal qualities, special talents and a lot of good karma.

However, a bad fairy sometimes comes to the new baby as well. This one casts the dark spells of negative past-life experiences. At their worst, these hidden influences can drain our energy with anxiety, depression, neuroses or phobias. They may also show up in the form of strange moods, unintended slips of the tongue and physical symptoms.

People sometimes experience negative past-life effects as an invisible block in their lives. They keep reaching for success or fulfilment. But like the main character in *Alice Through the Looking Glass*, they just go round in circles, always ending up back where they started.

In the twentieth century, psychologists found the magic key to solving these issues. They found that the best way was to regress their patients back to when the problem began. As soon as people knew that, the issue lost its unconscious power over them. After that, their old symptoms melted away.

This is why regression can break the dark spells that would otherwise haunt people throughout their lives. And it's not just a theory. Countless case studies have shown how effectively it works.

Hiding from the soldiers

Renate came for a regression because she'd suffered from claustrophobia all her life, and wondered if there was a past-life cause for it.

She went back to a seventeenth-century life during the English Civil War. She was hiding from enemy soldiers in a farmhouse. The soldiers suspected she was there, and kept coming back to search the place again. Every time they came, she had to scramble into a tiny, dark cellar under a trapdoor. She'd wait there in breathless terror till they'd gone. One night the soldiers found her there. They dragged her out, took her away and killed her. This was the origin of her fear of small, enclosed places.

Afterwards Renate told me that the guesthouse where she was currently staying had a small, windowless bathroom. Before the regression, because of her claustrophobia, she hated having to use it. The evening after the regression she enjoyed a relaxing bath in there without any of her old fears coming up. Her claustrophobia had lost its grip on her as soon as she understood where it had come from.

How does regression work?

Consciousness is like a multi-storey building. Everyday awareness is akin to one of the floors. When we're on that level, we can see only what's on that floor.

To find out what's on the other floors, we have to change to another level of consciousness. Regression provides a stairway between the floors.

It always begins with relaxation techniques to slow down the brainwaves. To do this, the therapist will talk in a calm, slow voice. They will often use images of soothing scenery and physical relaxation. Repetition and counting down also work well.

But all of this only works if the person is willing. If someone doesn't want to be relaxed, then nothing can force them into it.

As our brainwaves slow down, our consciousness changes. This is how we move to the other levels.

In the grand structure of our psyche, there are four main levels of consciousness: beta, alpha, theta and delta. They each have their own light, medium and deep levels. We go in and out of all of them every day and night as we move between waking, working, relaxing and sleeping.

We know this because these different states have been researched and measured using electroencephalograms – EEGs for short. Our brainwaves produce an electrical impulse and, to trace it, sensors are placed on people's heads, connecting them to EEG monitors. A wavy line on a graph then reflects their changing levels of consciousness. As they relax, so does the line on the graph, which becomes softer and smoother the deeper they go.

The four main stages of consciousness

Beta: This is everyday consciousness. We're in a light beta state when we're doing a routine task that requires our attention but isn't too demanding. Medium beta would be when we're studying, or trying to fix something.

A more intense focus – trying to hurry through heavy traffic for example – will take us to higher levels of beta. This level can also bring feelings of stress and anxiety. The beta line on an EEG graph is shallow and spiky, like a choppy sea.

Alpha: This is more relaxed. We slip into a light alpha state easily and naturally when we're daydreaming, listening to music or staring out of the window. The EEG graph line has bigger and more rounded curves, which look like a peaceful rolling sea.

Meditation or regression will take us to deeper levels of alpha. When we get there, we're at the gateway to the subconscious. At this level we can access material that's normally hidden from the everyday mind.

Studies have shown that past-life information becomes available when brainwaves measure around 7 to 8 cycles per second – which is the medium-to-deep alpha state.

Theta: We pass through theta just before going to sleep and in the first moments of waking up. The deeper states of lucid dreaming, trance and visionary experiences become available at this level.

Delta: This is deep sleep. In delta, we can access higher consciousness directly, and may be out of the body altogether. When we return to lighter levels of consciousness, we have dreams translating those experiences. Dreams are vital to us. When deprived of dream sleep, people experience mental breakdown and eventually, death.

We move naturally between these four levels of consciousness all the time. Being able to do this is important for our psychological and physical health and wellbeing.

Most frequently asked questions about regression

Why do people have past-life regressions?

There are four main reasons:

1. Because of a problem that they feel might have a past-life cause.

2. To seek a positive past-life memory that will be helpful or inspiring.

3. To follow up on clues they already have about their past lives.

4. Simple curiosity to see what past lives they might have had.

Can everybody be regressed?

In my experience, 98 per cent of people access past-life memories in some form. The very few who get absolutely nothing may be blocked for one of three main reasons:

1. It may not be the right time. A regression is an important part of the spiritual journey, and timing is key. This is why it's best to go for a regression only when it feels like a good thing to do.

2. Unconscious fear of what may come up.

3. Distrust of the whole process. This can come from fear of the powers of the unconscious and/or believing that only the 'rational' mind can be trusted.

How do past-life memories come up?

Everyone's regression experience is unique to them. There are no right or wrong ways. Past-life memories will come to you in whatever way is right for you. The key is to stay relaxed, trust the process and don't try too hard.

You may get:

1. An overview, with glimpses of several lives.

2. One life revealed in great detail.

3. A focus mainly on the emotional effects.

4. A few past lives around one theme.

5. A strong sense of inner knowing.

6. Images from your past lives like pictures on a wall or in a book.

7. Someone talking to you about a past life.

How can I be sure that I'm not making it up?

Your intention is the key. You will get what you intend to get. If you want to access a real past-life memory, then that is what will come up for you.

Even if you did try to 'make it up', your story would still contain truth about you because it came from *within* you. One of my workshop exercises is to ask people to 'make up' a past life spontaneously and share it with the group.

They're always surprised afterwards when they realize that they didn't choose a wonderful fantasy. Instead, they talked about ordinary lives such as a Victorian servant, a Roman soldier or a medieval farmer.

Talking it over afterwards often shows that clues about those lives were already in their current life. It becomes clear that although they set out to 'make up' a past life, they came up with a real one.

On this subject hypnotherapist Dr Morris Netherton said, 'Some patients start by feeling that they are "making up" parts of what they tell me. But they soon discover that they cannot change the content of their past-life incidents, and must reveal the most personal and painful aspects of the stories they had thought were imaginary. This is what most quickly convinces the sceptic.'

Another validation comes from the strong emotions that often arise during a regression. This creates involuntary physical effects, such as a reddening nose and tears. Reactions such as these can't be faked.

As psychologist and hypnotherapist Dr Edith Fiore said, 'Are they putting on an act? If so, most should be nominated for Academy Awards. After thousands of hours observing regressions, I am convinced there is no deliberate, nor conscious, attempt to deceive.'

Why do people so often think they have had famous past lives?

When people first hear about past lives, they often wonder if they were ever important or famous.

They may have a feeling that they lived in a particular time in history. Then they project that feeling onto an iconic figure who represents that era. A regression will often reveal that they did indeed have a life at that time – but not as the person they imagined.

For example, Annie wondered if she'd been Mary Magdalene. She'd had all kinds of dreams, flashbacks and synchronicities about that biblical world. Her regression showed that she really had been part of the new spiritual movement that was flowering in the Middle East at the time Jesus is believed to have lived and died.

She discovered that, as a young girl during that life, she'd decided to leave behind what she saw as her old frivolous ways. She'd joined a group similar to the Essenes and had dedicated herself to a life of spirituality instead. Although she hadn't been Mary Magdalene, it was easy to see why she'd had that impression.

Sometimes people identify with outstanding historical figures because of what they represent. This quality will often be something that they need to develop in themselves. In this way, the psyche uses fantasy to lead people towards their future potential.

Harold came for a regression because he'd received all kinds of signs supporting the idea that he was once Edgar Cayce, the famous American psychic. His regression showed nothing of the kind.

But in the second part of the session, his spirit guide told him that the idea had come to him because he needed to believe in and develop his psychic powers. The Edgar Cayce fantasy was not literally true – but it had a serious inner purpose.

Have you ever wondered if you were once someone famous? If so, don't dismiss the idea too hastily. It may not be literally true. But if you dig a little deeper, you may find that it was the outer wrapping of an important inner gift for you.

What if a memory that is too unpleasant to handle comes up?

During a regression you don't hallucinate or forget where you are. You can talk to your therapist as clearly as at any other time. So it's easy to say that you don't want to see any more. A responsible therapist will then move you on immediately – either to a more pleasant memory or out of the session altogether.

If you're getting the memory by yourself – through meditation or a self-regression CD for example – all you have to do is open your eyes, and you'll be back in your present world.

What if stuff that I don't want to talk about comes up?

You can simply keep quiet. Although it's more helpful for your therapy if you do discuss what's coming up, there's no obligation to talk about anything if it will make you feel uncomfortable.

You can also let your therapist know that you want to observe what arises, but without talking about it. And whenever you wish, you can ask to be moved to another memory or brought out of the session altogether.

What if I find out that I was a bad person?

Everyone on Earth has made all kinds of mistakes in their past lives. Nobody can point a finger at anyone else. We learn and grow through our mistakes. By the time this kind of past-life memory comes up, you've moved on from who you were in those days.

The memory comes up because it's time to forgive your past self and heal the effects of that life. Owning this kind of memory also enables you to move ahead with greater compassion and understanding for both yourself and others.

Is there any danger of becoming stuck in the regressed state?

None whatsoever. It's a natural state of relaxation, which you'll come out of whenever you feel ready.

In the past, people assumed that everyday consciousness was all that we consisted of. But we now know that different states of consciousness are a natural part of our human make-up and heritage.

Because of these discoveries, past-life knowledge may one day be an integral part of everyday life. Knowing how it works, we'll be able to access helpful past-life memories whenever we need to.

SUMMARY

- Regression is completely safe. It's natural and healthy to go in and out of different stages of relaxation every day and night.

- Regression works by slowing down your brainwaves. You'll be deeply relaxed, but still fully conscious. That level is all you need to access the real past-life memories that are held in the subconscious.

- Many of our current life issues come from past-life experiences. Understanding how they began is one of the best ways to free ourselves from a wide range of problems.

- Regression can also help us to understand more about ourselves in positive ways. It can remind us of happy memories and reconnect us with aspects of ourselves that will help us in our lives now.

- Discovering past lives through regression not only releases us from the past, it can also heal the present and create a better future for us.

Chapter 3

Secret Clues Around the House

As every advertiser knows, our homes, possessions, clothes, cars and general lifestyle all give out powerful signals about us. They reveal not only our status in the world, but also how we see ourselves – for example, regardless of wealth or social standing, a timid woman will always dress more drably than a young rebel.

How we see ourselves comes partly from the kind of world we were born into in this life. But a lot of it also comes from other lifetimes. Clues about those lives are around us all the time.

Deep down we know that happy past-life memories are a healthy influence. We therefore unconsciously surround ourselves with reminders of our best lives and experiences. These could have been times of abundance and security, emotional contentment, great achievement, learning or spiritual growth.

Even if we don't consciously remember them, those experiences are a great source of confidence, resilience and optimism. This is why we instinctively put physical symbols of them around us. They help us to draw that positive energy into our current lives. It's a bit like putting framed certificates on the wall to remind yourself and others of what you've achieved and who you are.

A pair of cowboy boots, for example, may cheer you up because they speak of a past life of freedom and adventure. An antique mirror might echo an elegant lifestyle you once enjoyed. A Persian rug may be a subliminal reminder of an intriguing life in the Near East. Retail therapy can run deeper than people think.

The home

The way we decorate our homes, as well as our tastes in furniture, pictures and treasured knick-knacks are all full of clues about our favourite past-life homes. If money was no object, what kind of home would you have? Given this choice, surprisingly few would opt for glittering palaces. Our ideal home is more likely to resemble a past-life place where we felt happy, safe or fulfilled – however humble it may have been.

The cottage

One of my clients told me that whenever she feels insecure or worried, she closes her eyes and imagines herself going to visit a cottage on the edge of a wood.

'It's always the beginning of autumn – still warm, with the leaves just starting to turn yellow. As I approach the cottage I see smoke coming out of the chimney. There are tall trees behind it.

'My grandparents live there. Grandpa's often working in the little vegetable garden at the back. Grandma's usually cooking nice things in the kitchen. I'm always welcome there. I don't even talk about my problems – I just go there to soak up their love and support.

'I'm sure this is a place I knew in a past life. This is probably why I've never wanted to live in a flat or even a large house. The home I have now is a lot like that cottage, and I love it.'

The harem

Terri told me that she's had several dreams of life in a harem. She feels sure this is about one of her past lives.

'It's quite a small place. There are only a few of us and we're all good friends. I feel safe and relaxed there. The world outside was dangerous and rough in those days. In the harem I was sheltered and protected. We were treated kindly. I enjoyed that life.

'It feels like it was somewhere in North Africa. I'm sure this is why I like things that remind me of that part of the world. I've got a tagine (a large, heavy North African cooking pot), which I always use when friends come round for supper. Those evenings are probably my way of harking back to my happy times in the harem.'

The yurt

Even a little night-light can have a big tale to tell. Glenda told me that she found it hard to sleep without its red glow switched on. One night she had insomnia, so she decided to gaze at the night-light to help her drop off.

'I started drifting, but was still partly awake. And I found myself in a big round tent – I think it's called a yurt. The night-light turned into the embers of the fire in the centre. I was lying on a pile of soft animal skins. It was so warm and comfortable. Other members of my family were also there, sleeping around the edges of the tent.

'It felt as if we were in some cold, northern country. I fell asleep gazing at the red glow of the fire. Some dreams came then. It looked like we were in Lapland. We wore Lapp-type colourful, patterned clothes, and had snow sleds. I think we herded reindeer. So now I know why I always wanted the night-light on. It reminded me of those cosy nights in the yurt.'

Do you have anything that hints of another time or place? When you look at your possessions with new eyes, you can make some surprising discoveries. Your everyday surroundings can become the door to some of your best and most empowering past-life memories.

Clothes

Often, we have favourite outfits and items of clothing that we like precisely because they unconsciously take us back to how we once were in an earlier life. For example, Gayle always had a kimono-style dressing gown. It was only years later she discovered that this was because she'd had a happy past life in Japan as the beloved wife of a wealthy man.

Similarly, Patti recalled life as a Quaker in the early days of America. She told me that some time ago she'd bought an antique dress from Dutch Pennsylvania. It made her feel strangely nostalgic. After the regression, she understood why – it was exactly like the kind of dress she used to wear in that life.

In contrast, Alana loved formal ceremonial dress. In her regression she discovered a past life in an oriental court, and later as a Renaissance princess. In those lives she loved the clothes – but learned to distrust large groups of people. She said this explains why she has never felt at ease when she's with more than a few people at a time.

And Jake realized that he loved wearing moccasins because they were a subliminal reminder of the magical things he'd learned during a Native American life.

Messages in fancy dress

In a way, all our outfits are a form of fancy dress. We put them together to show the world who we are and how we wish to be seen. Even if we aren't fully aware of it, this can also include elements of who we were in other lives.

One of my clients regressed back to a life in a monastery. Afterwards he mused that he now knew why he always went to fancy-dress parties dressed as a monk. It was because it felt normal and comfortable for him to dress that way.

Another client, Margot, went back to a life as a wealthy man in the sixteenth century. He'd fallen in love with a serving girl. The rigid social codes of the time meant that they could never marry. Whenever he went to visit her, he wore a suit of deep red velvet – perhaps as an expression of his love for her. After the regression, Margot told me that a few months previously she'd chosen a costume for her husband to wear to a fancy-dress party. She'd dressed him in a suit of red velvet. After her regression she realized that it was just like the one she used to wear in that past life.

The court jester

In classroom play readings Frank always got the part of the comedian. In one school play he had to wear the traditional jester's outfit of motley colours with cap and bells. He said that for some strange reason he really hated wearing that outfit.

In his regression he discovered a past life as a court jester. This life went to the core of his current problem. He had to decide whether to speak out about something important in a serious way that might backfire on him – or to stay safe by pretending to make light of the matter. In his past life as the jester he'd faced the same problem, risking real danger if he spoke his mind. But he decided to follow his conscience and speak out.

'I packed my things so I could leave quickly if I had to. I then dressed as an ordinary person. I went to see the lord of the castle. There was no one else in the room, just him and me. I was very afraid. But I told him what I felt I must.

'There was a long silence. Then he said that I was right not to wear my jester clothes any more, because that life had just ended. I thought that meant he was going to kill me. But instead, he promoted me to be one of

his advisors. It was the biggest relief I've ever felt!

'That's why I hated putting on the jester costume when I was a boy. It represented taking a step backwards. It meant being a coward and playing it safe.'

The past-life clues in your wardrobe

Take a look in your wardrobe to see what clues to your past lives you can find. The following questions may help to prompt your memories:

- Do you have a favourite item of clothing?

- Does it remind you of another time or place?

- What kind of person might have worn it?

- How do different outfits make you feel when you wear them?

- What kind of person would you like to be when wearing those outfits?

- If you could wear anything you like, what would you choose?

- What would you wear to a fancy-dress party?

Jewellery

Often standing for something significant from a former life, jewellery can represent past-life status, special qualifications or important triumphs.

Take Leila, who loved wearing a chunky brass necklace that she'd picked up on a tropical holiday. One night she had a dream that explained why she liked it so much. She was leading a religious ceremony somewhere in South America – and wearing an almost identical necklace. Whenever she looked at pictures of ancient Incan artefacts, she said a cold shiver of recognition ran down her spine. She realized that she'd been wearing that brass necklace to remind herself that she'd once been a high priestess there.

Brooches may be the echoes of medals or badges of honour from earlier lives. Hilary had a strange little brooch in the shape of a scimitar. As soon as she spotted it on a market stall, she knew she had to have it. When she came for a regression, she found out why it was so important to her.

She recalled a life as a young man in the Middle East, hundreds of years ago. Devoted to his spiritual path, he joined a secret esoteric school. He advanced steadily through all its stages of initiation. When he reached the highest level, he was given a jewelled scimitar as a sign of high attainment. Hilary's little brooch was a reminder of this achievement.

Rings often stand for commitment and responsibility. Tina had worn a moonstone ring for as long as she could remember. One day I asked her why it was important to her. She held the ring in the palm of her left hand with her eyes closed for a few minutes. Afterwards she said it represents her past-life commitment to 'the moon path' – the study of secret wisdom and magic. She realized that wearing the ring now was a sign of her continued dedication to that path.

Do you have an item of jewellery that feels especially

meaningful to you? Like Tina, you can find out more about it by holding it in your hand, closing your eyes and seeing it in your mind's eye.

As you do so, information or scenes from a past life may start to come up. If it doesn't work at first, don't be discouraged. These abilities are inborn in all of us and it just takes practice to start using them.

SUMMARY

- Our homes, possessions, clothes and even our lifestyle are full of clues about our past lives. We unconsciously pick things that will remind us of our best and happiest experiences.

- When you know what to look for, you can decode the clues that have always been hidden in plain sight in your everyday surroundings. Once you've made a conscious link to those positive energies, they become even stronger and clearer.

- Looking for clues around the house is one of the easiest and most enjoyable ways to draw beneficial effects from your past lives into your life here and now.

Chapter 4

Children's Past-Life Memories

A hospital pharmacist once told me that when she was four years old, her family took her to a museum exhibition. There she saw a display of mummies from ancient Egypt.

'It made me so angry,' she said. 'They'd been moved from their sacred places. It was all wrong to show them like this.'

As she grew up she forgot about that incident. Then one day, just out of curiosity, she came for a past-life regression. It brought back her childhood reaction to the museum exhibition – and made it clear why she'd been so angry.

In ancient Egypt she'd been a priest, in charge of mummification rituals. This was a highly important and holy task. The Egyptians believed it made a major difference to the afterlife of the departed spirit.

In that life she'd done a lot of research into the healing power of animal secretions. This was potent knowledge, which she said is now sadly lost to the world.

She realized that this was why she'd chosen pharmacy as a career. In her clinical white coat she was continuing the sacred work of an ancient Egyptian priest.

It's not unusual that her strongest inkling about that past life came to her at the age of four. Through the breakthrough research of the Canadian-American psychiatrist Professor Ian Stevenson, who carried out extensive studies about reincarnation, we know that children often can be in touch with their past lives.

Visiting the old home

Young children chat about their past lives in casual ways that are easy to dismiss as fantasy. In the twentieth-century Western world, if a child of four mentioned his old job, or his wife and children, it would usually be ignored as childish prattle.

But Professor Stevenson found that parents in India took this kind of chatter more seriously. As a result, he was able to verify several cases that began with a child talking about their 'other' family.

Those children were quite clear that they were talking about real people who lived elsewhere. They often had a good idea exactly where that was. They could help to direct the search and would recognize their old home when they got there.

Sometimes they pointed out real changes that had taken place since they were last there. For example, when little Swarnlata saw her old house again, she asked what had happened to the veranda and the neem tree. The amazed family said that both had been removed some years ago.

One of the old men in the house was Swarnlata's husband from her previous life. She immediately recognized him. To prove it really was her, she reminded him of the box of 1200 rupees that she'd once given him. Astonished, he said that only the two of them had ever known about that.

In another case, it was the cushions that did it for young Mallika. As soon as she saw them, she declared, 'I made those!' They had been made by a woman called Devi – who had died 10 years earlier.

Professor Stevenson's research confirmed that children can provide real and verifiable information about their past lives. This not only tells us a lot about childhood – it also validates reincarnation itself.

Children may also remember how they died. Sometimes this gives them a phobia about it. For example, Parmod had died in a bathtub and now hated being in water. Children's games can be their instinctive way of healing that kind of phobia.

The sea battle

Edward told me that when he was a little boy he liked turning his bed into a ship. He'd then fight off imaginary attackers in a desperate sea battle. He said that at around the age of six or seven he played this over and over again.

A few years later, he became fascinated with seafaring tales. On a school trip to Madame Tussaud's in London, his classmates couldn't pull him away from the ship-board scene of Admiral Nelson's death.

Old-fashioned schooners still sail through his dreams now and then.

'I've since found out that I had a past life as a sailor,' he said. 'I died in a sea battle. But I've never felt bothered about ships or water or gunfire. I think my little ship game somehow got all that out of my system.'

Many games that children play may have a similar hidden purpose. When put together with other clues they can tell us a lot – not only about our own past lives, but those of our children as well.

The past-life clues of childhood

Past-life memories usually start coming up between the ages of two and four, and fade between the ages of five and eight.

When children are in touch with a past-life memory:

1. They seem more adult and talk in a more mature way.

2. They speak about the memory in a matter-of-fact way.

3. Their recalled experiences stay the same whenever they retell them.

4. Some memories may be very vivid – especially if they're the cause of a current fear or phobia.

5. There may be birthmarks or deformities that relate to a past-life experience.

6. The child has traits, interests and preferences that don't seem to come from their current family.

7. They may have an inexplicable like or dislike of another country or culture.

8. They show signs of having skills or knowledge that they haven't learned in their current life.

Pulled out of the well

The following case ticks enough boxes to sound real.

'My nephew Jake is four years old,' said Vivienne. 'We were doing some sightseeing, and we came across a well. As soon as Jake saw it, he rushed up to it, and said "Uncle Rick was in here! I had to throw him a rope. I pulled him out."

When the family later returned to the same place, Jake had exactly the same reaction to the well. The adults asked him at different times if this is like one of his dragon stories – a fantasy.

'No!' was his adamant reply every time. 'This is real.'

Vivienne said the unusually mature and consistent way he talked about this incident convinced her that he was telling the truth. In a previous incarnation, it seemed that he really had saved his uncle's life by pulling him out of a well.

Child prodigies

Socrates said that genius is no accident. Outstanding abilities come from many lives of training and practice. The definition of a prodigy is a pre-teen child with a talent as good as or better than adults in the same field. The world usually gets to hear about the outstanding ones, such as Mozart. But there are probably countless children with all kinds of abilities from past lives that don't necessarily lead to world fame.

Kathleen told me that when she was three years old she used to draw a line on the floor, and then try to walk along it. It felt important to keep doing this. When she grew up, she discovered that in a past life she'd been a tightrope artist.

Her strange little childhood game finally made sense. The importance of keeping in practice had been so deeply instilled in her that she'd kept it up even in the early years of her next life.

The piano player

Researcher Joe Fisher wrote about the day Mr and Mrs De Felitta of Los Angeles will never forget. Relaxing by their pool, they were puzzled to hear ragtime music coming from the house. When they went inside to investigate, they were shocked to find their six-year-old son, Raymond, playing the piano like a professional. He had never even touched the piano before. 'My fingers are doing it by themselves!' he cried. 'Isn't it wonderful?'

At the time, his parents felt too disturbed to agree. His father said it was as weird as if they'd found their son suddenly flying around the room.

With his parents' eventual bemused encouragement, Raymond grew up to become a successful jazz musician. His style was similar to that of Fats Waller – who had died in 1945.

The twins from Minoa

When Beccy told me that she'd had a twin brother, I remarked that twins are sometimes people who were very close in a previous life. She said that was certainly true about them, and poured out the following tale:

'When I was about 12, I became obsessed with the Minoan culture. I mean, really obsessed. I ran out of children's books on the subject and started using the teachers' library. They got worried about me and told me to drop the whole thing. That was tough. But I did what I was told.

'Maybe it was just as well they didn't know what my twin brother and I used to play at! It was always horse tricks. I'd climb up a tree. He'd then get the horse to come under the tree. When it was just below me, he'd yell, "Jump!" and I'd jump down onto the horse.

'When he grew up, he joined the Royal Navy. One day he announced that he was going to fight in the Falklands War. Before he left, he said he might not come back. He put all his affairs in order. And he was right – he didn't come back. It was very hard for me to lose him.

'Years later I was on a meditation retreat. One of the men there – someone I'd never met before – suddenly said, "You had a twin".

'We went into a quiet room to talk. He told me that my brother and I had lived in ancient Minoa. We were part of a team that did acrobatic acts riding on the bulls.

Our lives depended on getting it right. The bulls' horns were deadly, so it was all about split-second timing.

'One of our tricks was for the girl – me – to be thrown straight at the bull's horns. The man riding the bull – my brother – would then catch me just before I reached the horns. That always thrilled the crowd.

'Well, one day he didn't catch me. The horns did instead and I died of the injuries.

'The man said that in this life my brother had come back to be with me to make up for that accident. It's also why we played those dangerous horse tricks when we were kids – we were re-enacting the bull riding. Doing that somehow healed the effects on both of us of the terrible accident we'd had in Minoa.

'I have no idea how a complete stranger could have known about that. But it made perfect sense. Everything fell into place at last.'

Mothers' dreams

Pregnant mothers sometimes dream about their baby's past lives. An American woman, Martha, told me that when she was pregnant she dreamed that in a previous life her baby was a Mafia mobster. He was coming to her because she was his best hope of returning to a happier way of life that he'd known with her in a much earlier time.

The dreams showed her that in this life he needed to do team activities with strong and positive role models that he could emulate. After some trial and error – he soon became bored with sports that weren't dangerous – he got into white-water rafting and rodeo riding.

Martha said her son is now settled in a happy career leading groups on eco-conscious safari trips. She feels sure that this is thanks to the dreams she had about him just before he was born.

The orphans

A mother's dreams about her children can be so strong that they go beyond one lifetime. In her book *Yesterday's Children*, Jenny Cockell described how a past-life drama spilled into the present.

It began with a recurring childhood dream. She kept dreaming that she was a grown woman called Mary, lying in bed, dying of a fever. After those dreams she'd always wake up crying. Her grief wasn't for the dying woman, but for her eight children who were about to be left alone in the world.

Those dreams haunted Jenny for so long that she became convinced she'd once been that dying woman. In some of the dreams she saw her past-life village so clearly that she could draw maps and pictures of it. She said it felt like somewhere in Ireland.

One day, she decided to find out. She scoured the records, eventually tracking down a woman called Mary Sutton, who'd died of a fever and left eight children.

Mary had lived in a small village near Dublin in the first half of the twentieth century. When Jenny went there, she said it was like her dream had come to life. The village was exactly like the maps and pictures she'd drawn of it.

With so much confirmed, her next step was to contact the eight orphans with her amazing news. Much older by then, they were doubtful at first about this stranger's tale, but they gave it a fair hearing. To their surprise, they found that Jenny knew private family details that no one but their late mother could possibly have known.

It looked as if their long-lost mother had indeed returned – and Jenny was able to put a lifetime of anxiety about them behind her at last.

Can you remember what you knew about your past lives when you were very young? That may not be so easy to recall now. But if you go through the following exercise, you may begin to unearth the past-life clues that your inner child has for you.

Exercise: Getting past-life clues from your childhood memories

Our childhood memories are full of clues about our former lives. Dressing-up games, our favourite periods in history, our unexpected skills and our loves and hates – all are rich sources of information. Following these clues can open up a pathway taking us back to the past-life awareness that we had when we were very young.

Choose a time when you can forget the demands of the world, and relax somewhere comfortable. Focus on one of the 10 key questions listed below. Let them waft you gently back to your childhood – and beyond. There's no need to rush this. One topic per session is probably enough.

In your childhood:

❖ What were your preferred activities or hobbies?

❖ What special events stand out?

❖ What were your favourite books, comics or magazines?

❖ What games did you play?

❖ Which subjects at school did you love or hate?

❖ Which films or TV shows made the biggest impact on you?

❖ Do you remember having any big emotional reactions about anything?

❖ What was your favourite food?

❖ What clothes did you love or hate to wear?

❖ Did you have any strong attitudes about anything?

When it feels like enough for one day, keep a note of whatever came up. As you progress, you'll be able to piece together all kinds of past-life clues from the secret garden of your childhood memories.

SUMMARY

- Thorough professional research has shown that young children are often in touch with their past lives.

- Under the age of eight, children talk freely about past-life memories. In many cases, the details they've given have been verified beyond doubt.

- There are more past-life clues in children's abilities, feelings and attitudes.

- Childhood games may point not only to former life experiences but also to their healing.

Chapter 5

Your Favourite Places

Reincarnation has its own geography. As the long path of our soul journey winds around the Earth, we build up all kinds of personal associations with particular places. Those bonds can be strong enough to continue calling to us over great distances of time and space. When we go back to those places, we often recognize them with a strong feeling of déjà vu – a deep inner knowing that we've been there before.

When Jeff visited Assisi for the first time, he had an extraordinary déjà vu experience. He knew exactly how the town was laid out, and found his way around easily without a map. He also remembered buildings that had once been there, but had now disappeared. He said it felt like he'd come home.

The writer Louis Bromfield was sure that his love of France came from an earlier life. 'Nothing ever surprised or astonished me there,' he wrote. 'No landscape, no forest, no château, no Paris street, no provincial town ever seemed strange. I had seen it all before. It was a country and a people that I knew well.'

Ever since childhood, the hypnotherapist Arnall Bloxham had vivid dreams of earlier times. One of those dreams came true when he visited the Cotswolds for the first time.

It began with a strong déjà vu feeling about a certain steep hill. In one of his recurring dreams he was always going down that hill in a bumpy coach – and feeling travel sick. Even though he'd never been there before, he somehow knew that at the bottom of the hill there'd be big iron gates between two towers.

That was the entrance to Sudeley Castle in Gloucestershire – which he instantly recognized as his home in a previous life. Once inside, he immediately knew where everything was. He was able to show his wife and friend around, identifying all the rooms and special features without a guidebook.

While the déjà vu experience gives us big clues about our former lives, there are also many other ways in which past-life places may call to us. The main reasons for this are:

1. To complete unfinished business.

2. To heal a negative past-life effect.

3. To strengthen a positive past-life effect.

Completing unfinished business

Over the course of our lifetimes, we leave all kinds of loose ends lying around the world. We may come into this life intending to find closure or healing for one or more of them. This could mean completing an unfinished journey, letting go of an old pain or keeping a promise to return somewhere one day.

Sometimes we don't have to travel far to do that. If it's important to be in a certain place for past-life reasons, we may simply be born there.

There can be many good reasons for being reborn in the same place again. For example, when a life ends suddenly, the spirit will often reincarnate very quickly in the same area. This makes it easy to pick up where it left off.

Wartime effects

In his previous life one of my clients was deeply involved in secret work during the Second World War. He was reborn near to Bletchley Park soon after the war. That was where they turned the course of the war by cracking the German secret codes. He's now still actively engaged in international peace work, continuing the mission of his earlier life.

Another form of unfinished business comes from a past life when an important journey failed. Despite all our desperation and determination, we just didn't get there. When this drive is strong, it reactivates in another life. We are then finally able to complete that journey.

The journey home

In a past life, Andy was an escaping prisoner of war. He was trying to make his way back from Germany to England. Unfortunately he was caught and shot while still halfway across Europe.

In this lifetime Andy was able to complete that journey. The chance came up for him to travel across Europe back to England. Although it wasn't as dangerous as his past-life journey, it was still tricky enough to make him nervous.

'It had its challenges,' he said. 'But I was much more jumpy than this trip warranted. It was only when I got on the ferry back to England that the fear began to ebb away. And when I saw the white cliffs of Dover, I was overjoyed.

'At the time, I didn't know why that journey had such a big effect on me. But now that I've had a regression, I can understand it. I was completing my escape from during the war. That's why it felt so good.'

Migration to America

Dr Roger Woolger, who specialized in regression therapy, wrote about his past life as a French Huguenot. After years of persecution, his family decided to join the wave of Huguenots migrating to the new world of America.

Sadly, by then he was an old man, and the journey was too much for him. 'I remember dying miserably by the roadside', he wrote.

But, as I think so often happens, his deepest wish came true in the end. In his next life, he was reborn in America. There he lived the free life of a trapper. He was able to enjoy all the liberty he'd once yearned for as an oppressed Huguenot in Europe.

Healing negative effects

We naturally associate unpleasant past-life experiences with the places where they happened. As a result, we may reincarnate with a strong distaste for those parts of the world. This is often coupled with an unconscious inner drive to go there again and heal that effect.

The mysterious boat journey

In her regression Alicia discovered a past life in Scotland. She was a Stuart supporter – on the side of Bonnie Prince Charlie and his doomed claim to the throne. The memory began with her standing on a quay, watching a battle. She felt utterly helpless.

When she went home she found that her house had burned down and her children were dead. And more attacks were on the way. She was bundled into a boat with the other survivors, to get away as fast as possible. They all went and hid on an offshore island.

She said it felt so wrong to leave her dead children behind like that. The grief and guilt she felt at the time were at their worst during the boat journey to the island.

In the second part of the regression, her spirit guide explained how the real purpose of her recent trip to Scotland had been to heal that memory. While there, she'd taken a boat trip from the mainland to an island. The little excursion brought up strong feelings in her, both joyful and anxious.

Her guide said the reason she'd been drawn to do that boat journey again was to heal the old pain. He said that she hadn't needed to feel guilty at the time and she could let it go completely now.

Sometimes we may need to heal the effects of banishment, exile or a sad migration. When we have to leave a homeland we loved, we often whisper a promise to ourselves that one day we will return. When we do so, even if it's lifetimes later, it brings us deep emotional healing.

This process can sometimes take strange twists and turns.

Forgiving England

A Dutch woman, Anneke, came for a regression to get to the bottom of her problems with her Anglophobia. She said at school she'd hated her English lessons and all her English teachers.

Then, in one of life's little ironies, she ended up marrying an English teacher. On top of that, he was an Anglophile – in love with all things English. Her son felt the same way. But she stubbornly refused even to speak English with them.

After years of this stalemate, she decided it was time to sort it out. While on holiday in England with her family, she came for a regression to get to the bottom of this issue.

She found that she'd been a Roman Catholic priest when Henry VIII made his break with the Vatican. He disbanded all the Catholic monasteries and grabbed their assets. Almost overnight it became dangerous to be a Catholic in England.

In that life Anneke tried to protest against this – and was killed for it. The fury she felt about this had gnawed away at her ever since. After that life she refused to incarnate in England again and chose to live in Europe instead.

After the regression, she realized that she'd been keeping her anger burning about something that was now irrelevant to her. She decided that it was time to end her self-imposed exile, and become friends with England again.

Back to Stonehenge

Carrie experienced a subtler form of exile. She'd gone to visit Stonehenge – and felt nothing but anger and hostility towards the place. So she came for a regression to see if there was a past-life reason for this.

She went back to a time when she was a female shamanic practitioner in that part of the world. It was a meaningful way of life, full of ancient wisdom and the mysteries of nature.

At that time, Stonehenge symbolized the beginning of a new way. It represented more mental control over religion, with greater male dominance. The people were impressed with the great new ceremonies. The old shamans and wise women were increasingly ignored and pushed aside. This was why she still hated Stonehenge.

Talking it over afterwards, Carrie said she couldn't see her way to resolving this issue. She wasn't ready to let go of her anger.

But a few months later, I heard from her again. She'd been back to Stonehenge to try and make her peace with it. While there, she'd gone into meditation. She was granted a sweeping vision of the many different good ways in which Stonehenge has served and helped people. One of those ways included help she herself had received from Stonehenge in a previous life.

'I'd gone there with some horrible illness,' she said. 'And the place somehow cured me. I was so happy and grateful. So I've decided that my earlier self needs to stop hating Stonehenge. I'm fine with it now.'

Strengthening positive effects

Places where we had happy, fulfilling lives may continue to call to us like an affectionate mother, wanting to nurture and look after us. Going to those places can feel welcoming as a home. These are the havens that we visit whenever we need to recharge our batteries.

Crete: my real home

'My childhood roots were in Yorkshire – but I've never really felt at home there,' a friend of mine once remarked. 'Strangely, I feel much more rooted in Crete. The first time I went there, I felt that I had come home. It feels like I belong there.

'Right from the start I knew my way around "my" patch of Crete. Every lane and corner was familiar. For practical

reasons, I can't live there at the moment. But I go there often. Whenever I do, I always feel better afterwards.'

We both felt this was because she'd had at least one happy past life there. Her Cretan holidays gave her the emotional strength that kept her going through some tough challenges she had to face. She feels sure that one day she'll go back to live in Crete – if not in this life, then in the next.

Return to Wales

Laurie yearned to live in Wales, but life kept blocking her from making that move. She wondered if this was due to a past-life problem, and came for a regression to find out.

She went back to the life of a Victorian Welshman, working on the railway. There was an industrial dispute. He spoke out in a hotheaded way – and lost his job. Because he'd been blacklisted, he couldn't find work again. He had to endure the guilt and sorrow of seeing his family beg for charity as he couldn't support them.

In the second half of the session, Laurie's spirit guide said this experience had cut her off not only from Wales, but also from her own voice. In that life, because of the terrible consequences it had had, she'd decided never to speak out again. This guilt also made her feel exiled from her beloved Wales. She felt that she didn't deserve to go back there.

We did some work on forgiving herself and getting her voice back. Less than six months later, both a job and a place to stay came up for her in Wales. It was suddenly easy for her to move there.

'The first day I was back there, I went for a long walk in the hills – and sang my heart out!' she said.

The pilgrimage

Many of us had key past lives in important spiritual centres. Revisiting those places reconnects us with the inner strength, clarity and wisdom we had while living there. While visiting ancient sites all kinds of clues and synchronicities about past lives there may pop up. People have also reported feeling back in touch with the knowledge they had in those times.

This can apply not only to ancient temples but to whole countries. Jo told me how happy she was to have 'got India back'. All her life she'd had dreams that were obviously set in India. But she had a love–hate feeling about it, and no wish ever to go there.

'Then one night I woke up after one of those dreams about India. I went back into the dream in a semi-lucid way. It showed me the places I'd been dreaming about. There were Mogul palaces, city slums and little villages in the country.

Someone was with me, explaining it all to me. He said in India I'd once lived a life of luxury, but I'd felt guilty about it at the time. In another life I'd lived in the slums and found that very hard. My happiest times there were when I was far away from palaces or cities.

'He said I needed to accept now that I'd had all those experiences for a reason. I won't have to go back to them again. I can be at peace with all of those lives now.'

Later Jo went on holiday to India for the first time. She loved everything about it – its swarming cities, grand palaces and tiny villages. She felt that her enjoyment was a sign that she'd finally made peace with all her past lives there.

The spiral path

Cultures throughout the world have used mazes and labyrinths as a symbol of the spiritual journey. The remains of an ancient spiral pathway are still visible today winding its way around Glastonbury Tor.

People who've trod that path say the old magic is still there. Peter felt that it reconnected him to a former Druid lifetime.

'Whenever life is getting too much for me, I walk that path around the Tor. It takes me back to a much earlier time. It was when I was more in touch with the magic of nature.

'It always feels as if I have a hooded cloak on. The material is quite rough. And I have the urge to chant. I don't want to call attention to myself, so I just hum quietly. But I can sense what it originally sounded like, and I listen to that in my mind.

'Walking the spiral path like that always restores my energy and refreshes my spirit.'

Exercise: Discovering your special past-life places

This is a light-hearted quiz to nudge your memories and spark off clues about the places you once lived in.

Sometimes an answer will come up straight away, as if from nowhere. Other times your mind may take you on a relaxed wander around the subject. Both ways will give you information about your past lives in special places.

Choose a time when you can be quiet and relaxed. Pick one of the following questions, and put it to your inner self. Then wait for words, images or feelings to come up.

❖ If you could live anywhere, where would that be?

❖ Go back to an important journey. What was the deeper reason for it? When and where did that journey really begin?

❖ Where would you like to return to one day?

❖ Which place in the world does your inner self most want to visit?

❖ Which place do you never wish to see?

❖ Which place has benefited your spirit the most?

❖ Where was your past life just before this one?

❖ Where have you spent most of your lives?

❖ Where was your first life on Earth?

SUMMARY

Strong feelings about any place in the world – whether positive or negative – are a good sign that you had a past life there. Other clues are:

- Dreams you've had about it.

- Signs and synchronicities that draw your attention to it.

- A déjà vu experience when you get there for the first time.

You may feel drawn to visit a special place to:

- Complete unfinished past-life business.

- Reconnect with work or studies you were doing there.

- Heal any negative feelings about that place.

- Reinforce the positive effects of happy or fulfilling lives there.

With this knowledge, you can pick past-life places to visit for the healing and inner sustenance they may have in store for you. Holidays may never be the same again!

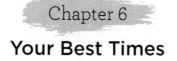

Chapter 6

Your Best Times

'The past is never dead. It's not even past' said author William Faulkner. There will always be certain times in history that live on within us through our past-life memories. Those special times are an important part of our spiritual journey. Because of that, our lives are full of clues about them.

Once you know how to spot those clues, it's easy to decode them. You can then trace the path that your soul has woven through the different cultures and customs of your mysterious journey through history.

Dreams in historical dress

Dreams set in historical periods are one of the biggest clues about the past lives we had in those times. They can also bring a message about how that life may be affecting us now.

The rescue

Althea had a vivid dream of herself as a young woman in the Middle Ages. It was night. There was an atmosphere of danger and urgency. An older man was helping her onto a horse ridden by a young man. Holding her close in front of him, he galloped away as fast as possible. That was the whole dream.

Althea recognized the young man on the horse as her present older brother. He'd recently been annoying her with what she felt was overly controlling behaviour.

The dream had come to show her why he was like that. He felt that it was his duty to protect and look after her. When she realized that, she was able to deal with him in a more understanding way, defusing the rising tension between them. He became more relaxed about her, and the gathering storm soon blew away.

The train

Wendell had to work with a group of people who were beginning to drive him mad with their rigid adherence to petty rules. During that time he dreamed of being in a train with them. They were a wealthy family, dressed in 1920s clothes. Wendell was their butler.

He said the train was moving at great speed through the twentieth century. Flashing by were images of the Depression, wartime London, rock-and-roll parties, mini skirts and flower-power hippies.

Next morning he realized what the dream was about. His irritation with the group had come from his past life with them. He felt that they looked down on him as a servant.

He also saw where their old-fashioned attitudes came from. But the rushing train meant they were leaving those ways behind and speeding into a new future.

Wendell found that understanding this made a great difference. He felt more confident and relaxed with the group and his relationship with them soon improved.

The plot

Felicity dreamed of being an eighteenth-century girl in a wealthy town house in France. A young man came and put poison into a coffee cup. She then took that cup upstairs to someone. The dream stopped at that point, so she never saw what happened next.

But she knew who the young man was – he was also in her current life. It was clear that this dream had come to warn her about him. She said he liked to poison people with gossip, but had always thought she was immune to it.

After this dream she realized that she might not be immune. She decided to break off the connection and felt greatly relieved when she'd done so.

Old allegiances

Clues about our lives in other times may also come out in the kind of causes and allegiances we continue to feel strongly about.

I once had a fascinating conversation with one of Oliver Cromwell's men. He explained to me how everything Cromwell did was good and why his enemies were wrong. I eventually put it to him that he may have had a past life in Cromwell's army.

This was a new idea for him. He stopped and thought about that for a few moments, while his wife nodded enthusiastically to me from behind him.

'You never know,' he eventually concluded. 'I might have. It wouldn't surprise me.'

Working with the past

People may express their attachment to past eras through their hobbies or their work. Writers of historical novels and films could be unconsciously drawing on past-life memories. The writer Joan Grant said that her historical novels about Ancient Egypt were actually stories from her past lives.

Museum exhibits can jog ancient memories in both visitors and the people who work there. Historians may specialize in the times they once knew first-hand in person. In their search for ancient artefacts, many an archaeologist could be unconsciously digging for their own past.

People may be drawn to work with particular times in history for one of the following reasons:

- A sense of mission to restore those old ways to the world.

- Personal unfinished business from that time.

- Loyalty to the leaders, causes or ideals of that era.

- A need to 'go back' to make up for something or put matters right.

- To recover something or someone they lost or left behind there.

Minoan ways

Some years ago, a friend sent me this e-mail:

'My cousin Frances is visiting Glastonbury this weekend. She's big on Minoan culture and lived on a Greek island for 12 years.

'She's writing and researching about the ancient Minoan civilization and is interested in meeting anyone with some knowledge of or interest in such things, while she's here.'

During her visit, Frances came to me for a regression. Unsurprisingly, one of the past lives she discovered was in ancient Minoa. In that life she was a woman who did administrative work. She wasn't important or rich – but it was one of her happiest lives because of the kind of world she was living in.

Minoan women enjoyed enviable levels of freedom and equality. This might have been because the Minoans placed great value on the 'yin' qualities of compassion, sensitivity and creativity. As a result, they lived in a joyful, gentle and beautiful world.

Years later, Frances told me that that particular lifetime was the source of more than just her academic interest in Minoa. It was also an inner touchstone for an ideal community that she'd been seeking. She realized that she'd always been on a mission to bring the civilized ways of ancient Minoa back into the world today.

The sceptic and the Cathars

History can have strange ways of catching up with us. Dr Arthur Guirdham, a psychiatrist working in Bath in the 1960s and 70s, was sceptical about anything but physical explanations for people's inner problems. Because of this, his nickname was 'Doubting Thomas'.

One day a new patient, Mrs Smith, came to see him. She told him that she was troubled by recurring nightmares of being burned at the stake. Of course, Dr Guirdham didn't mention it to Mrs Smith, but for years he'd been having exactly the same nightmare.

That was only the first surprise she had in store for him. As her treatment progressed, she began to remember in great detail her past life as one of the Cathars, a medieval heretical religious sect. Reincarnation was one of their core beliefs. They did especially well in the Languedoc region of France, where they were known as 'albi gens' – 'the good people'.

When the Church saw how they were growing in popularity and influence, they decided they were a threat. So between the Albigensian Crusade and the Inquisition, they wiped them out. Hundreds of Cathars were burned at the stake. It makes sense that even lifetimes later, people who'd experienced this in past lives would still be having nightmares about it.

During her sessions with Dr Guirdham, Mrs Smith provided many highly specific details about those times. She could remember people's names, what had happened to them, the songs they'd sung and the kind of clothes they wore.

Dr Guirdham started looking these things up to see if he could verify them. He dug deeply into a lot of obscure historical archives. He also consulted Professor Nellie, who was the greatest living authority on that period in history.

Between them, they verified every single detail that Mrs Smith provided. The Professor was deeply impressed. He told Dr Guirdham that in future, if there was ever any conflict between the historical view and the memories of his patient, he should 'go by the patient'.

But Mrs Smith's biggest bombshell was for Dr Guirdham himself. She told him that he'd also been a Cathar – and they'd known each other in that life. She even remembered what his name had been.

That explained why he'd also been having nightmares about being burned at the stake. This was a major life-changing event for the once sceptical doctor. It transformed his entire outlook and he went on to write several books about past lives and the Cathars.

His conclusion was, 'If I didn't believe in reincarnation on the evidence I'd received, I'd be mentally defective.'

The anniversary syndrome

While he was going through his transformation, Dr Guirdham discovered the anniversary syndrome. He found that if a major event had taken place in a person's past life, when the date on which it had happened came round again, the person subconsciously knew it. As a result, strange dreams, nightmares and unexplained strong feelings were likely to surface on that date.

For Dr Guirdham and Mrs Smith the trigger date was 16 March. In 1244 they were living at the Cathar centre of Montsegur when the Pope's army besieged them. On 16 March, they chose death by fire rather than renouncing their 'heresy'. Dr Guirdham realized that this was why their nightmares about being burned at the stake were always at their worst around that date.

Holidays and Birthdays

Because of the anniversary syndrome, public holidays, religious festivals, seasonal celebrations and even our own birthdays can all be magnets for our memories. Past-life dramas that happened on those days may wake up and whisper to us again whenever those dates come around.

A Diwali candle

Although Miriam had been brought up in the Jewish faith, she had always felt drawn to Diwali – the five-day Hindu Festival of Lights. When it came round every year she lit a special candle. She said that doing so helped her to feel part of it in some way. Until she came for a regression, she had no idea why she felt so strongly about Diwali.

She went back to a life in India as the daughter of a poor family. When she grew up, she and the son of a wealthier family fell in love. His parents opposed the match for a long time. But they doted on their only son, and he persisted, so eventually they gave in.

When the couple married, the first festival they celebrated together was Diwali. Every year after that, she dedicated Diwali to thanking the deities for all her blessings. This was why it still meant so much to her – even before she knew exactly why.

The anniversary syndrome can apply to your age as well as to special dates. If something big happened in a past life when you were a certain age, that memory may be revived when you reach the same age again.

The lost Christmas

After his 32nd birthday, John turned against Christmas. He said it was because he'd suddenly realized that it was all so materialistic. But when he dug deeper one day, he discovered that at the age of 32 in a past life he had lost a beloved child.

That Christmas had been so miserable without the joy of his child that he decided never to celebrate it again. Because this decision was so heartfelt it faithfully kicked in again in this life when he reached the age of 32.

When death walked away

One of my clients, Clara, told me that some years ago she had suddenly had a strong impulse to lock herself in the bathroom, where she'd be private and undisturbed.

Once there, she lay down on the floor and closed her eyes. She was instantly transported back to a medieval battlefield.

'I saw Death come and peer at me to see if I was ready for him,' she said. 'He was exactly as he appeared in those old pictures – a skeleton in a ragged cloak with a giant sickle.

'But it wasn't my time to go with him. He shook his head and went away. Two soldiers then came. They put me on a stretcher and took me off the battlefield. After that it faded.'

When she came for a regression, Clara discovered that in Scotland hundreds of years ago she'd been one of the leaders in a battle. The man she was in that life was badly injured and taken off the field exactly as she'd recalled.

After a long time he recovered from his wounds. But he could never fight again. He'd fought his last battle in that lifetime. It happened at the same age Clara was when she had that strange vision in the bathroom.

At that age, Clara's life had also taken a new turn. She'd given up a high-flying career to become a farmer's wife.

'That was difficult for me at first,' she said. 'I felt so isolated. I also saw myself as useless because I wasn't

doing important work any more. It must have been how I felt in that life when I had to stop being a warrior. Maybe this is why I had that flashback.

'But later on I got over those feelings. I found that my new way of life was full of good things. I'd never go back to the old way now.

'And now I also know that my Scottish warrior did the same thing. He got over not being able to fight again. He felt good about becoming a wise advisor instead.

'I wonder now if I linked up to that past life because we've been helping each other in some way. We both needed to let go of an old way of life. We both had to find the good in a new way. Maybe it was easier for me to do that in this life because I'd already done the same sort of thing.'

Issues from our past lives can sometimes come back to us in a new way. But as we progress, they get lighter and easier to deal with. Our past selves, who walked that path before us, help us to get through the rough patches. They may come to us with the strange clothes and quaint ways of bygone times – but the gifts they bring are timeless.

Exercise: Tracking your past-life clues through time

As with all of these exercises, the best way is to treat them as a fun game. It's not about getting correct answers. The questions are simply signposts for an enjoyable journey of exploration.

Pick a quiet time when you can be relaxed. Choose one of the following questions. Imagine that you're sending it to your inner sources of wisdom. Close your eyes and wait for images, feelings, thoughts or ideas to start coming up.

Afterwards make a note of whatever came up. When you look back over your notes one day, you may be surprised at how many pieces of your jigsaw are starting to fit together.

- ❖ What is your favourite historical era?

- ❖ What do you like most about it?

- ❖ If you could go back there, who would you like to be?

- ❖ What sort of life would someone like you have had in that time?

- ❖ Do you feel strongly one way or the other about any public holiday?

- ❖ How would you ideally like to spend that holiday?

- ❖ Has any particular date or birthday ever had a special effect on you?

- ❖ What are your favourite historical films or novels?

- ❖ Which historical outfit would you choose for a fancy-dress party?

- ❖ Have you ever had any dreams set in historical times?

SUMMARY

- Dreams set in historical times will usually be about a past life. The dream will often have a message for you about how that life is affecting you now.

- Feelings for or against different historical periods are clues about your experiences in those times.

- Strong loyalties or anger about old causes are signs of past-life involvement with them.

- Work or hobbies that focus on particular periods in history may also point to lives lived in that time.

- Anniversaries of important past-life events can bring echoes and reminders of them back into our lives.

- Challenges we faced in a past life sometimes come back in a new form. Our past-life experiences help us to deal with them.

- Understanding these connections helps us to heal the past, transform the present and create a positive new future for ourselves.

Chapter 7

Your Talents and Abilities

'Genius is experience,' Henry Ford once famously said. 'Some seem to think that it's a gift, but it's the fruit of long experience in many lives. Some are older souls than others, and so they know more.'

Edgar Cayce said it takes 35 lifetimes of training to produce a genius. But we don't need to wait that long to have a past-life skill. Most people have something they're good at, and which comes easily to them. These inborn abilities spring from the learning and experience of earlier lifetimes.

Our talents, skills, abilities and even hobbies are therefore full of clues about our former lives. This doesn't mean we are stuck with doing the same old things for all time. Part of the unfolding story of our lives is how we develop old skills to use in completely new ways.

From stables to the board room

In her childhood, Emily loved drawing pictures of race-horses. Although she never bothered to bet on them, as an adult she enjoyed watching horse races on television.

When she came for a regression her connection with horses became clear. In a former life, she'd been the wife of a racehorse owner. She'd been fully involved in her husband's work and had learned a lot in that world.

Afterwards she said the skills she'd gained in that life were now coming in handy in a completely new way. She explained that she worked in the human resources department of a major organization.

'There's always an undercurrent of company politics going on there', she said. 'It's unspoken of course, but I know about it anyway. I think that instinct comes from my life in the world of horse racing.

'Now I can always tell the difference between what people say and what they really mean. In that life I learned a lot about horses – but much more about people!'

The artistic monk

Greg came for a regression because there seemed to be an invisible block in his life. Although he was an expert technical artist, he couldn't find any work in that field. He'd ended up working in a shop. He wondered if there was a past-life reason for this.

In his regression he went back to a life as a monk. By the light of one candle, he was doing the intricate artwork of illuminated manuscripts. He loved his work. It had important spiritual meaning for him. He was also very good at it.

Then disaster struck. The monastery burned down. All his precious life's work was lost. This had a major impact on him. He wondered what the point was of ever trying to do anything. He also feared that the fire was a punishment for taking too much sinful pride in his work. As a result, he never went back to illuminating manuscripts. For the rest of that life, he just worked in the monastery herb and vegetable gardens.

In our discussion afterwards, Greg said that in this life he's always had an ambivalent attitude towards his artistic skill. He dropped out of art college before he completed his course. Whenever anyone complimented him on his talent, he could never accept it.

He said the regression made it clear where his artistic abilities had come from. It also showed why he's been so blocked about them. Now that he knew the cause of the problem, he felt able to deal with it.

Shortly after the session, he e-mailed me, describing a series of meaningful synchronicities that had unfolded for him later that day. His magical day included an unexpected visit to Glastonbury Abbey.

'Maybe there was a deeper reason and I was meant to go to the abbey,' he wrote. 'I was drawn to the abbey's herb garden and orchard. One thing I read struck a chord. The current abbey was rebuilt in the early thirteenth century, after an older building was burned down in 1184.

'I wonder if my monk had lived at the old abbey – and if that was the smoking ruin I saw in the regression?

Maybe I was drawn to the herb garden and orchard because that's where I ended up working.'

Greg decided to get back into his art by treating it as an enjoyable hobby. He felt that allowing his creativity to flow freely again would be the best way to reclaim and develop his past-life talent.

Sometimes recalling a past-life ability is all we need to confirm a path we've already set out on, but may be feeling nervous about.

The herbalist

In her regression, Gwen went back to medieval times. She was living happily with her husband, who was a farm labourer. Within a few years, however, the Black Death had killed him and her children.

It was a devastating experience for her. She had no idea how she was going to support herself. The only skill she had was a knowledge of medicinal herbs that she used for her family. So she decided to see if she could sell her herbal concoctions.

She went to a local fair, found a quiet corner, and spread her wares out on a cloth on the ground. But far from helping her, the local people showed her nothing but hostility. They accused her of being a witch, saying she'd murdered her husband with sorcery. The women kicked over and trampled on all her medicines.

It was time to leave. With her meagre belongings in a bundle, she walked away. She said that even then she somehow knew that she would survive. (Later she told me that she'd woken up that morning with the song 'I Will Survive' on her mind.)

After some searching, she eventually found a place where the people accepted her. She settled down in a little cottage and was happy. She spent the rest of her life making herbal cures for the villagers. They were grateful for her help and she felt loved again.

In the second part of the session, Gwen spoke with a spirit guide about this memory. He said it came up to remind her that her spiritual work had turned out well before, and will do so again. Although she's afraid of being attacked again, she will be safe this time.

Afterwards she told me that she's continuing the work she did in that life, in much the same way. But she had always felt uneasy about it. After this session she said she felt reassured and relieved.

A week or so later, I had this e-mail from her:

'I thought you might be interested to hear about a synchronicity that occurred a couple of days after my regression with you.

'You'll probably remember that in my past life, I went to a local fair in a field to sell my potions and herbal remedies. Because of the hostility of the local women, I laid my cloth and medicines out in a corner of the field. I thought I might be left alone there.

'Among my remedies was a bottle of precious oil. When the local women did arrive they kicked over my

potions, including this oil. It felt as if my life-blood was flowing away with the oil.

'As my friend Jenny and I made our way home after our visit to Glastonbury, we discussed this. She wondered what the oil had been. Immediately I said "Marigold". I have no idea where that came from. I know nothing about marigold oil.

'A couple of days after we got home, Jenny texted me to say that her herbal book had fallen open on a page saying that Henry VIII had used marigold to ward off the plague!

'After doing an internet search I saw that the first record of marigold being used in this way was in the fourteenth century. That was when the Black Death decimated much of Europe.

'I feel that a change has occurred within me since my session with you. I can't put my finger on it precisely, but it has something to do with self-confidence.'

The memory came up for Gwen to let her know that it would be safe to continue her herbal work. Despite the setbacks she went through, it had turned out well in the end, and would do so again. On top of that, her intuitive flash about the marigold oil gave her an extra boost of faith in her inner knowing.

Maybe that's where all the confidence we gain in our abilities is ultimately leading us – towards a trust in our own innate wisdom.

Signs of your abilities from a past life

The five signs of abilities from a past life are:

- Childhood games, fancy dress or fantasies about any skill or job.

- Your favourite hobby.

- Anything that you're naturally good at and find easy to learn.

- Skills or abilities that you love to use.

- Any subject that you feel drawn to, and which is easy to understand.

SUMMARY

- Abilities that we learned in a past life are never lost. They will always be a part of us, and can be revived if it suits our current path.

- Knowledge that we gained in previous lives remains within us. Those memories can be a source of inner knowing about many different subjects, making it easy for us to learn again.

- Problems about using an ability or talent may arise from a difficult past-life experience. This can be resolved when we understand what happened. Using that skill again will then be part of the healing.

- Skills from an earlier life can be adapted and updated, so that we can use them in a completely new way.

Chapter 8

The Biggest Triggers

Past lives can sneak up and jump out at us just when we least expect it. We may be enjoying a movie, reading a book or doing a bit of leisurely sightseeing when suddenly our world feels like it's been turned upside-down.

Something has triggered a past-life memory – and when that happens, it's like letting the genie out of the lamp. It won't go back, and you can't ignore it. From then on, it will be part of your life. It may not grant you three wishes, but if you pay attention to it, like the genie it will bring some new magic into your life.

Movies

Because they're designed to immerse us in their world, movies are one of the best triggers for past-life memories. When that happens, the memory that's been dozing in our subconscious suddenly wakes up and gives us a prod.

The emotions we felt at the time are usually the first thing to come up. Flashes of the actual memory may then follow.

We may also get a strong sense of inner knowing that we once lived in that kind of world.

I was there!

In 1936 an incident took place in a Liverpool cinema that startled not just one person but the whole audience. The movie was showing the beheading of Lady Jane Grey, who was queen for just nine days in Tudor England. Suddenly a young woman in the audience shouted out 'It's all wrong! I was at the execution!'

Afterwards she said she suddenly knew that she'd been a lady-in-waiting at that event. Her memory of the executioner was especially clear. She said he wore black bands around his wrists as a sign of his grim office. They weren't part of his costume in the movie – like many other details she said were incorrect.

These days, when a movie reminds us of a past life, we're less likely to be quite so startled by it. We probably won't leap up and blurt things out. We're starting to take this kind of effect more in our stride – but it can still be unexpected.

A friend of mine went to see an acclaimed Chinese movie about concubines called *Raise the Red Lantern.* She said it hit her so hard that she wandered around the streets of London for hours afterwards. That was her way of absorbing the impact of realizing that she'd just seen something very like one of her own past lives.

Conspiracy in the monastery

When Stuart came for a regression he found, as many others have, that he'd been a monk in a past life. He discovered that the monastery was full of dark secrets. As he tried to expose them, he put himself in mortal danger.

One day he had to take a message to another monastery. On the road there, two brigands attacked and killed him. He knew the Abbot had sent them to do this.

Afterwards he said he now understood why the movie *The Name of the Rose* had had such a strong effect on him. It had haunted him for days because it had reminded him of his own dark experiences in the monastery.

Regency days

Susannah told me how much she loved films of Jane Austen's novels.

'I can watch them over and over – I don't really care about the story,' she said. 'I just love feeling like I'm back in that world again.'

Her love of delicate textiles, long dresses and formal manners also pointed to her penchant for those times. She felt that the modern world has become coarse and chaotic since then.

So it was no surprise that when she came for a regression, she went back to a life in Regency England.

The real surprise was that she'd been a faithful old servant to a large household.

The family she worked for were kind and had treated her well. Because of that, she'd put them and their whole way of life on a pedestal. They were an ideal that she longed for and aspired to – not just in that life, but in this one as well.

Books

Books can be major triggers of past-life memories, widening our inner horizons and opening doors that we never knew were there.

Sometimes those books can be part of a healing process as well.

The great escape

When Rod was a teenager, all he wanted to read was World War Two prisoner-of-war escape books. No other kind of war story interested him.

When he came for a regression, he discovered that he'd died while trying to escape from a German prisoner-of-war camp. The searchlights found him as he ran away, and the guards shot him.

He felt that the books he'd read about escaping prisoners who'd got away had somehow helped him to get over that death. Regressing back into that experience was like taking the dressing off an old wound – and finding that it was healed.

What Finny did

When Finny was a child, she loved Susan Coolidge's *What Katy Did* books, set in America in the late nineteenth century. She said she began to write imitation stories of her own, about a large and happy family living on America's East coast about a hundred years ago.

She'd naturally forgotten all about her stories until she came for regression. Then she discovered that she'd lived in exactly the kind of family she'd depicted at that time in America. Triggered by a book, the stories she wrote as a child had been drawing on her own memories.

'I wrote it all down in a notepad of bright-pink, lined paper,' she said. 'I can see it in front of me now. I'm sure I must have thrown it away as rubbish later on. It's strange to think how that silly-looking notebook actually had some real significance.'

The wreckers

Stephanie came for a regression to see if she could sort out a problem with a work colleague. She told me there was a strangely deep hostility between them. She didn't understand it and wondered if it might come from a past life.

In her regression, she went back to a life a few centuries ago. She was one of the men who used to loot ships that had been wrecked in storms and washed ashore. They also used to lure ships onto rocks to destroy them, for the same purpose.

Her memory began at a sea cove. The man she'd been was wearing a tricorn hat and black shoes with buckles. A ship had been wrecked, and the gang was waiting to grab its bounty. A chest had already come ashore. They opened it with a crowbar and found treasure inside.

Sailors from the wreck were also washing up on the shore – some of them still alive. The gang's usual policy was to kill any survivors, to stop them reporting what they'd seen.

'This time, I decided not to do that,' Stephanie recalled. 'There's a woman, her cloak flapping in the wind, who's yelling something. She's my wife. She's very angry because I didn't order the men to kill the sailors. She says they'll tell on us.

'She yells, "You're a fool John Mosset! I'll show you what a man looks like!" And she grabs a stick and goes and bludgeons the half-drowned sailors to death. The others just shrug. The general feeling is, it needed to be done.

'When we get home she's screaming with rage like a banshee. She tries to hit and kick me, saying she never liked me and she regrets marrying me.

'After she's screamed herself out, I go outside to think. I make up my mind that it's time for me to leave her – and also this whole way of life.'

So he left and found his way to London. To make up for his past he later became a gentle priest, much loved by his flock.

Afterwards Stephanie said the furious woman in that life was the work colleague who'd been giving her so much trouble. She decided to try one last time to make peace with her. But if that didn't work, she'd do the same thing – wash her hands of it and walk away.

She also told me that she had at home a library book called The Wreckers. She'd felt very drawn to it – but once she'd got it, she couldn't face reading it. Nor could she bring herself to take it back to the library. She'd had to renew the library loan three times without ever opening it.

The next time Stephanie came to Glastonbury, she told me that after the regression she'd found it easy to read that book. She discovered it was about exactly the sort of thing she used to do – looting wrecked ships. But knowing that she'd walked away from it in the end made it easier to read.

When she went back to work, she heard that her troublesome work colleague was getting a transfer elsewhere. The problem had solved itself.

'I wonder how this works?' she asked. 'It looks as if just becoming aware of the past-life cause of a problem somehow helps it to melt away.'

Pictures

It's said that if you stare at a picture for long enough, it will feel as if you've entered it. But to be an effective trigger of past-life memories, lengthy gazing may not be necessary. If the picture rings a bell for you, just one look can be enough.

The Viking

The following experience happened to a friend of mine when he was a little boy.

'I used to get the children's educational magazine Look and Learn,*' he said. 'One day it arrived on the front doormat as usual. I picked it up. On the cover there was a picture of a Viking. He was in full battle regalia, with one of their ships behind him. And I fainted! No other picture had ever had that effect on me – not even the gory, violent ones.'*

When he came for regression other, more pressing memories came up. It clearly wasn't the right time for him to access his Viking memories. But other clues in his life are like the tip of that hidden iceberg.

He told me once that he'd suddenly thrown out all his son's books about Vikings. And over the course of his life he's spent a lot of time in Scandinavia. This may be part of a healing process centred on that part of the world – where the Vikings originally came from.

The German portrait

Life may even present us with a portrait of ourselves in a previous life. In his book *Past Lives, Future Lives*, hypnotherapist Dr Bruce Goldberg writes about a woman who went on holiday to Germany. While she was looking around an old German castle, she saw a thirteenth-century portrait on the wall.

She stood in front of that picture completely transfixed for 45 minutes. She'd recognized the picture as herself in a past life. As she stood there, all her memories from that time came tumbling into her mind.

'The Blue Boy'

One of my clients went back to a life that confirmed something he'd long suspected – he'd been the model for Thomas Gainsborough's picture, *The Blue Boy*.

He said that the first time he saw the picture he was transfixed. He knew with every bone in his body that he was looking at himself in another time.

In his regression he had an overview of several lives, with brief glimpses of each. One of them was in eighteenth-century England, a life that he began in wealthy circumstances but later fell on hard times. This supports what we know about Jonathan Buttall, the model for Gainsborough's picture.

A theme ran through all the lives he was shown. It was the tension between enjoying being the centre of attention and wanting to get away from it. He often became cynical about how fickle admiration and popularity can be.

By this lifetime he'd developed a deep distrust of people. He said getting these memories helped, because he could now see where that issue had come from.

Next time a picture from long ago draws your attention, look a bit closer. Scenes that feel strangely familiar may be showing you the kind of world you once lived in. If a portrait of someone from the past rings a bell for you, you may or may not have been that literal person. If not, you could well have been someone a lot like them.

SUMMARY

- There are all kinds of triggers that will wake up past-life memories.

- The most common triggers are movies, books and pictures.

- You can tell if it's a past-life trigger by how it makes you feel. A strong and sometimes puzzled reaction is a good sign. It means that a past-life memory may have begun to surface from your inner depths.

Has anything ever rung a bell like that for you? If so, that bell may have been one of your past selves asking to be let in. They come to us when we're ready for them. Once we accept them – even if some healing is needed – these aspects of our greater self can become our best allies.

Chapter 9

How the Body Holds Past-Life Memories

The spirit body is our real self. It goes from one physical body to the next, carrying with it all the memories and experiences that it went through in previous lives.

When your spirit takes on a new body, it's like putting your hand into a glove. As a glove takes on the shape of a hand, the new physical body is shaped by the spirit that inhabits it. In this way, past-life experiences get imprinted onto the new body.

This is why the physical body holds and expresses past-life memories in so many ways. It also explains why understanding the past-life cause of a physical problem can lessen and often completely heal it.

Psychologist Dr Edith Fiore maintained that past-life treatment is the best way to help any physical problem, saying 'Other therapies address the symptoms and leave the cause untouched. Past-life therapy attacks the root cause.'

Although we naturally pay more attention to the negative physical effects, our past lives can also endow us with health, strengths and physical abilities.

For example, Felicity was bored with her clerical job. She loved going to her evening dance classes, but regarded that as just a pastime.

When she came for a regression, she discovered that in a nineteenth-century life in France she'd been a ballerina. This was why dancing came so easily to her.

This revelation got her to rethink her priorities. She realized that in this life she'd never wanted to go back to the rigidity of ballet. But she did like the fluid movements of Latin American dance. So she decided to make a new life out of that. Within a year she'd changed her job from bored clerk to happy dance teacher.

Posture and gestures

Our posture and mannerisms can express habits and attitudes from earlier lives. For example, an upright bearing can come from a former life in the military. Someone with a hunched, weary look could once have been heavily burdened or beaten. Finding it easy to sit cross-legged on the floor may point to past lives spent in meditation.

The subject of one of Professor Stevenson's case studies said that she recognized her reincarnated sister because she still had exactly the same way of independently striding ahead of everyone else.

Mannerisms from past lives can show up in all kinds of unexpected ways. And as Emily found, they can sometimes be surprisingly helpful.

The submissive lady

When Emily came for a regression, she began by talking about glimpses she'd had of a medieval life in a castle. As she talked about this, she held her hands folded up into her chest. It seemed a quaint, archaic sort of gesture, so I asked her about it. She felt that it was to something to do with that medieval life.

In her regression she found that she'd chosen that particular life to develop certain qualities to strengthen and balance her inner self. She'd had some wild lives before then, but now needed to learn the opposite ways – to become quiet and compliant. This was how a lady in a castle was meant to behave, so it was perfect training for her.

Of course, she doesn't need to be meek and medieval any more in her current life. But she said that whenever she has to be patient or accepting about anything, she automatically folds her hands over her heart. When she does so, the strength she gained in her medieval life comes back to her. Like a true friend, it has helped her through many different situations.

Physical reminders

The body has many ways to remind us of our past lives. Sometimes a similar physical experience will be all we need to trigger a vivid memory.

The formal peach

One day Charlotte sat down to eat a peach. For a change, she took the trouble to use a nice plate, and cut the fruit into neat slices. She said as soon as she tasted that peach, vivid memories came to her of a formal Chinese life she'd once had.

She recalled wearing elaborate robes. Although she was a woman with no obvious power, she had a lot of real influence. At the time, this felt as far as possible from Charlotte's circumstances.

'I think that came up to remind me of a part of myself that I needed to remember,' she said. 'I'd been feeling quite low and disempowered before then. This turned me around. That peach fed my soul as well as my body!'

The icy hands

Andy was washing some mushrooms in icy water. Although his hands were freezing, he felt it was important not to stop. Then a flash memory suddenly came to him of a past life when he was frantically trying to dig someone out of a snowfall.

'The pain in my hands was intense but I had to keep going,' he said. 'I realized that my hands had gone back into the snowfall experience. That's why I was feeling so driven about it. As soon as I recognized that, I stopped and warmed them by the fire!'

Body marks

The body marks that babies are born with often have a past-life tale to tell about them.

Psychiatrist Professor Ian Stevenson found hundreds of children with birthmarks that looked just like the scars of fatal wounds that they'd received in their past lives. The birthmarks appeared on the body exactly where the blow had fallen. They also looked like the kind of wound that was inflicted. For example in a previous life, Ravi's throat had been cut. He had a birthmark across his throat that looked just like the kind of scar a knife would leave.

Pitnov had once died from a spear wound in his abdomen. His current body had a birthmark in exactly the same place. It was the perfect shape for a spear wound. This also explained his phobic fear of knives. Whenever he felt tense, the past-life wound would play up and he'd have pains in that area.

Towards the end of his life, William George, an Alaskan fisherman, said to his son, Reg, and daughter-in-law, 'If there's anything to this rebirth business, I will come back and be your son. You'll recognize me because I'll have birthmarks like the ones I have now'.

Five years later he died at sea. Soon after that Reg's wife fell pregnant. Shortly before the birth she dreamed that her late father-in-law appeared to her. He said he was waiting to see his son, Reg, again.

Her baby was a boy – and had the same birthmarks in exactly the same places as her father-in-law's had been. The couple was convinced the baby was the old man reincarnated, just as he'd predicted. They called their new son William George Junior.

Movement

Sometimes past-life effects can create rigid ways of moving and holding ourselves. The psychologist Wilhelm Reich called this 'armouring', because our muscles act like a suit of armour that keeps us stuck in old patterns.

Dreams of clowns

Pete began to have a series of dreams about clowns. He came for a regression to see if this was about a past life. However, the past life that came up was just the opposite. It was one in which he'd been rather a severe priest.

When we delved deeper into the clown dreams, it turned out that they'd been trying to release him from the stern priestly ways that still hung around him like a black cassock.

In the dreams the clowns were always floppy and loose-limbed. As we discussed this, Pete understood their message to him. He needed to make that kind of movement to release himself from his old dour self. Understandably, he wasn't ready to try it out then and there, but said he'd work on it.

Some weeks later he e-mailed me, saying, *'I went to some exercise classes, but they weren't right. I needed to do something that was much more free-flowing. I couldn't find it anywhere – so in the end, I just started doing that by myself at home.*

'I imagined myself as one of the clowns from my dreams, and just lolloped and flopped around in a silly

*way. I always felt really great after doing that. I think
I must have had a past life as a clown – and it's come
back to save me from turning into a complete nerd!'*

Using movement and dancing can heal and restore us by shaking off old patterns that our body may feel stuck with. It can also remind us of earlier happy times.

Angie had always been rather timid, and no good at standing up for herself. But after she took up Scottish dancing, she began to blossom.

At that time she started having dreams about a rough Scottish woman from hundreds of years ago. That woman had all the confidence and chutzpah that Angie needed. The dancing had reminded her body of how she'd once been. From then on it was easy to leave her shy ways behind.

Exercise: Dealing with the past-life cause of a physical problem

Pains or problems in any part of the body may have come from a past-life experience. In this exercise you can find out more about it and help to alleviate it. Choose a time when you'll be relaxed and undisturbed. Do your favourite relaxation exercises. Then go through these 10 steps:

1.   Describe what the pain or problem is like.

2.   Imagine what kind of thing could have caused it.

3.   Allow images to come into your mind about that.

4.   Get one clear image of an event that could have caused the problem.

5.   Once you have that clear image, see it crumbling into dust.

6.   See a fresh wind blow it all away, scattering every speck far into the distance.

7. Clap your hands sharply to finally dispel all the after-effects.

8. Stand up and have a good stretch, fully expanding your body.

9. Take a few deep breaths, expelling the air in a big sigh through your mouth.

10. See the golden light of health filling your whole body.

SUMMARY

- The body is like a book about our past lives. When we know its language, it becomes easy to read. And when we know how to read it, we can also help to rewrite it. In this way we can heal ourselves of many physical effects that come from our past lives.

- Birthmarks often have dramatic stories to tell about past lives and deaths.

- Physical experiences can trigger similar past-life memories.

- Posture, mannerisms and movement reveal a lot about our former lives and experiences.

In all these ways and more, our bodies can bring in past-life aspects of ourselves to help us in our current lives.

In Chapter 11, I go into the past-life connection to physical ailments. The body may carry old wounds and sorrows, but when we understand its secrets we also access its great power to heal those wounds.

Chapter 10

How to Find Your Past Lives

The first time that many people hear about their past lives is when they go for a psychic reading. This kind of brief introduction is just enough to make them curious. The next step is usually booking a regression to find out more.

There are, however, a number of other ways to explore your soul history. This chapter is an introduction to the best of those methods. They are safe and fun to experiment with, and will show you many different ways to look at your past lives.

Dowsing

Dowsing is easy to do and available to everyone. You don't need any special skills. It does use psychic energy, but that energy comes through you into the pendulum or dowsing rod. Dowsing comes from a well-established, time-honoured tradition. For centuries people have been successfully dowsing for underground water, oil, metals, precious stones and historical sites. To do this, the dowser most often uses a forked stick, holding one prong in each hand. With the stick pointing straight ahead and level to the ground, the dowser moves slowly over the area. When the stick suddenly wrenches downwards of its own accord, it means the object of the search is directly below.

Sometimes two L-shaped metal rods are used. The dowser holds the short ends, with the long ends pointing directly ahead. This kind of rod is especially sensitive to unseen forms of energy, such as the human aura. They react by swinging widely open or closed.

To access past-life information, a pendulum is probably the best dowsing tool to use. This can be any small weight suspended by a chain, but a crystal will give the best results.

When you've found a pendulum that you like, the first step is to find out which way it will swing for 'yes' or 'positive' and which way for 'no' or 'negative'. Hold the end of the chain in your left hand, and wait for the crystal to hang in stillness. Then say 'show me a yes'. You can reinforce that by holding it over a piece of paper with the word 'yes' written on it.

It could then start to swing from side to side, back and forth, or in a circle. A circle usually means that the answer is uncertain or ambiguous. But some pendulums may move in clockwise or anticlockwise circles for 'yes' or 'no'. When you've found out how your pendulum will indicate a 'yes', repeat the same procedure for the word 'no'.

Then try it out by asking 'yes' or 'no' questions that you know the answer to, such as 'Is today Sunday?' When you and your pendulum are working happily together, you can then move on to your journey of discovery.

To follow are some methods that you can experiment with to help you find out about your past lives.

Dowse a map

Hold your pendulum over a map to find out where you had a past life. Try different places on the map. Each time, say out loud or clearly in your mind, 'Did I have a past life in this place?' Give your pendulum time to settle and react before you move on to the next area.

Dowse the body

Ideally, you need two people to do this – one to lie down while the other does the dowsing.

In the same way as dowsing a map, move the pendulum little by little over the person's body. Pause often, each time asking, 'Are past-life memories held here?' Remember to dowse the back as well, because many unconscious issues are held there. The shoulders, arms, hands, legs and feet are also important – but any part of the body can be affected.

Dowse your possessions

Most of us have things we've bought or that have found their way into our lives – things that subconsciously remind us of our past lives. They could be jewellery, ornaments, pictures, clothing – even large pieces of furniture.

Pick something that feels significant. Then hold your pendulum over it and ask, 'Does this have past-life meaning for me?'

Dowse pictures or photographs

If you're wondering about possible past-life connections with certain people or places, you can dowse pictures of them. Hold your pendulum over the picture and ask, 'Do I have a past-life connection with this person/place?'

When you've established a past-life connection with a place on a map, in the body, among your possessions or with someone you know, you can then go on to ask more questions about it.

Begin with these four core questions as your foundation. You can then ask new questions that occur to you, depending on the answers the pendulum gives you. Frame all your questions to have a 'yes' or 'no' answer.

For example, ask yourself: 'Did that life take place in the twentieth century?' If the answer is 'yes', ask if it was in the first or second half of the century. If the answer is 'no', ask if it was within the last 500 years. Continue refining your questions until you get a 'yes' answer.

Once you've established a clear time in history, you can even find out the year of your past-life birth by asking about specific years until you get a 'yes'.

Here are some more questions to ask:

1. In that life, was I:
    – male?
    – female?

2. Is that life still affecting me now?
   - yes?
   - no?

3. Is that life affecting me in:
   - a positive way?
   - a negative way?
   - in both negative and positive ways?

4. Does that life affect my:
   - health?
   - relationships?
   - work?
   - finances?

Once you have the answers to these basic questions, you can continue getting more details until you have a good picture of that past life.

Dowsing can tell you a lot about your past lives and what you can do to either heal or enhance those effects.

Astrology

Some parts of the astrological birth chart are specifically about past lives and can be useful tools to explore them. It's easy to get your birth chart done on the internet, often accompanied by helpful interpretations. Because many of the charts are free, you could download a few and compare the results.

These are the three aspects of your chart that refer to past-life effects:

1. The south node: the past to be left behind

This is about the ingrained habits, negative effects and old patterns from your past that are now holding you back. It may point to abilities from earlier lives, which now need to be either left behind or transformed in some way.

2. The north node: The future to grow towards

This is about your highest potential. It's the inner purpose of this incarnation and represents the best path you can take in this lifetime for your personal growth.

For example, my south node is in Virgo. This refers to past lives that were focused on analytical work. My north node is in Pisces, which is about intuition and mystery. So my purpose in this lifetime is to learn to rely less on left-brain skills and take a more mystical path instead.

On looking back, I can see how perfectly that has unfolded. While at university, I seemed all set for an academic career. But my life took another path altogether. I became fascinated by all things spiritual and other-worldly. Now, although analytical skills are still handy, I see them as one of the many tools that we can use to progress along our spiritual path.

3. Retrograde planets

A retrograde planet in the birth chart can be a positive or a negative thing. If it's positive, it will be about someone or something from a past life that it would be good to revisit. If it's negative, it will be about things from the past that need to be left behind.

You can find out if the retrograde planet is positive or negative by looking at its aspects to other planets. The charts that you download will give you this information.

For example: if Venus is retrograde, positive aspects could mean that a past-life soulmate is destined to come back into your life. Negative aspects might be about a past love holding you back in some way.

A badly aspected retrograde Mercury could mean having to amend something that was said or written in a past life. If the aspects are positive, it might mean picking up on studies you began in earlier times.

A retrograde Mars that has bad aspects might point to the need to heal or let go of past-life conflicts. But if it's well aspected, it could be about positive dynamic influences from former times returning to help you now.

Astrology won't show the exact details of your past lives. But it will give you a meaningful overview of your soul journey. This is a useful addition to the more comprehensive past-life knowledge that you can unearth in other ways.

Crystals

Crystals carry specific vibrations, which help all kinds of inner work. You can hold them while meditating, wear them as jewellery or carry them with you in a protective pouch.

Below are seven of the best crystals for helping you to recall and heal your past-life experiences:

1. Apatite: for accessing both past and future lives.

2. Apophylite: to help you find your past lives in the Akashic Records.

3. Cerussite: to explore past lives away from this planet, and to help you understand why you incarnated here this time.

4. Moldavite: especially effective when held on the third eye, in the middle of the forehead. This helps you to see into both the past and the future. It gives a meaningful spiritual view of past lives rather than the factual details.

5. Herkimer Diamond: good for attuning consciousness to a high level. Helps to clear the chakras (the body's subtle energy centres) and gently release old blockages from past lives.

6. Serpentine: excellent for forgiving yourself and others. It will also help you to recall the between-life worlds.

7. Wulfenite: heals any inner wounds caused by past-life persecution for believing in magic. It also helps you to recognize the people you have a soul contract with in this life.

Dreams

Dreams are excellent ways to find out about your soul history. You can tell which dreams are about your past lives: they're the ones that are set in another time or in a part of the world you've never visited.

These dreams come to us for good reasons. If you have a dream like this, it means your inner spirit wants you to become aware of it because it will help you in some way.

Here are four good ways to understand past-life dreams:

1. Keep a dream diary

Write down everything you remember about the dream. If you keep a regular dream diary the clues will build up and you'll be surprised at how much information you gather.

2. Go back into the dream

Do so with the intention that you're going to find out more about it and understand what it means.

Quieten the mind by relaxing and breathing slowly and deeply. Then focus on the dream. Imagine yourself in that place again. Notice all the details around you. Try talking to the people in the dream and see what you can find out from them.

With a bit of practice, this method can be a good way to discover the inner meaning of every important dream you have.

3. Incubate a dream

This means simply telling yourself that you will have a dream to answer a question. You could ask for a follow-up dream to tell you more about a past-life dream you've had. Or you could ask for a new dream about a past life.

Incubating a dream is like telling yourself to wake up at a certain time in the morning. Your inner self hears and will do as you ask. The dream you've asked for will come to you quite soon – if not that night, within a week or so.

In the meantime, keep a notepad by your bed so that you can write down the details while they're still fresh in your mind.

4. Learn the language of dreams

All dreams talk in symbols. Every object in a dream has meaning and significance. For example, a table is never just a table, it represents how people gather together. A past-life dream featuring an expensive-looking table would be about an elite social world. A plain wooden table represents a more ordinary situation. A table for two will stand for a special relationship.

Bags are another important symbol in dreams, as they refer to our main occupation. In a past-life dream, the bag you carry will tell you a lot about that life. For example, depending on what it looks like, a bag could represent a life of fun, of penury or of study.

To give another example, dream shoes signify your path through life. Sandals often represent spiritually centred lives. Clogs point to a simple way of life. Shiny boots mean being higher up the social ladder.

Dream dictionaries can be helpful. But in the end, every symbol in your dreams is personal to you. This is why one of the best ways to understand them is by free association. Ask yourself what a dream object reminds you of, then what that reminds you of, and so on. This is one of the quickest and most direct ways to translate a dream.

Guided visualization

Guided visualizations are both easy and enjoyable. They'll work just as well whether you experience them in a talk, a workshop or from a CD, book, phone or Skype session.

This method works because it keeps the mind pleasantly occupied, while at the same time taking us to deeper levels of consciousness. As with dreams, the images that come up will be more about inner meanings than literal details. The soul talks to us in the language of symbols. Knowing that makes it easy to understand whatever may surface during a guided visualization.

Self-regression

This is a way of using meditation, relaxation and guided visualization techniques to help you find past-life memories for yourself.

The three keys for success at this are: intention, relaxation and trust.

1. Intention is important, because you will get whatever you really intend to get.

2. Relaxation is vital. To access deeper information, you need to be relaxed to slow down the brainwaves.

3. Trust is also essential. If you distrust this process, your abilities or your own inner self, it will be difficult to accept whatever may come up.

Stage 1: Intention

This means simply deciding that you want to get a real past-life memory. Your inner spirit will hear this, and respond in a genuine way. The more you trust that, the easier it will be.

Then think about what you're looking for. For example, you might want a memory that will:

1. Show you the reason for a current situation.

2. Help you to make a decision.

3. Be personally beneficial for you.

4. Show you an ability that you can reclaim or develop.

5. Reveal your current life purpose.

For additional reassurance, you can also ask your guardian angels and spirit guides to be with you to help and watch over you during the session.

Stage 2: Relaxation

Each of these tried-and–true techniques works quickly and will relax you whenever you need it. You can use as many or few of them as you prefer, in any combination that works for you.

When done before any kind of meditation, visualization or exercise, these techniques will get you better results. When practised regularly, they'll give you a greater sense of permanent inner peace.

Movement

Try the following:

1. Slough off the cares of the world by shaking your hands and feet.

2. Do head and shoulder rolls to soften the tension that gets held there.

3. Clench and unclench your muscles a few times, especially in the face, shoulders, arms and hands.

Toning

Toning helps to unblock the energy meridians within your body. Repeating the well-known 'om' (pronounced 'ah-oom') is excellent, because the vibration of this sound creates higher harmonic patterns that radiate through your whole being.

Feel the support under you

Focus on wherever your body is touching the floor, chair, bed, or sofa. Notice every detail of how it feels. Enjoy the feeling of how comfortable and supported you are.

Breathing

Take a few deep breaths, letting them out like big sighs. Then start to breathe slowly and deeply. Quieten the mind by listening to the sound of your breath.

Relax your muscles

Imagine relaxation flowing through your whole body. Let all your muscles soften and feel heavy.

Soft music

Choose a soothing piece of music and immerse yourself in it. Let it waft away all your concerns and help you to drift into a pleasant state of relaxation.

Focus on an object

Gaze steadily at a mandala, a candle or a crystal. Think of the object as a symbol of your calm inner centre. Let go of all other thoughts.

Sound

Still the mind by listening to every sound that is going on within and around you. Although the sounds of nature are ideal, this exercise works just as well with any kind of sound. Even the whoosh of passing traffic can be soothing when we use it like this.

A beautiful place

Close your eyes and imagine yourself relaxing in a beautiful place – perhaps floating in a warm sea, lying on soft green grass or basking in the sun.

Mantras and affirmations

Mantras are words or phrases that calm the mind when repeated over and over again. Use a positive affirmation, such as 'I am relaxed, centred and confident.'

Stage 3: The journey

When you feel relaxed enough to go on your journey, you will have three vehicles to choose from. Each one will show you different types of memory.

The magic carpet

This will take you to a physical past life that you had on Earth.

Imagine that you're relaxing on a beautiful magic carpet. It's comfortable, stable and strong. It knows which memory would benefit you the most to know about. As soon as you're ready, it will take you straight there.

You can then stay on the carpet as it moves from scene to scene. No one there will be able to see you. You'll be able to observe invisibly everything you need to know from that lifetime. Unless you wish to, you won't have to re-experience anything.

When you've seen enough, the carpet will bring you back. Alternatively, anytime you want to return, you can simply open your eyes.

The cloud

The cloud will show you a spiritual overview of your past lives. As you relax, imagine yourself floating on a beautiful white cloud. It's soft and comfortable, but will also support you firmly.

The cloud will know what would be best to show you. As soon as you're ready, it will take you to a place where you can learn more about your soul journey.

When you're ready to come back, it will bring you safely home. Again, anytime you want to come out of this meditation, it's fine to just open your eyes.

The space bubble

This will help you to explore memories from other worlds, other dimensions or between lives.

As you relax, imagine yourself in a tiny spaceship for one. It has huge all-round windows, like a flying bubble car. Although you can see out, no one can see in. You're completely safe and protected as it floats gently through the beautiful regions of other-dimensional space.

It will take you to the other-worldly memories that would be the most helpful and enlightening for you to know about. You'll be able to observe invisibly from inside the bubble.

When you're ready to return, you can either open your eyes, or let the space bubble bring you safely home.

SUMMARY

You can learn more about your past lives using a number of different methods:

- **Dowsing:** You can get past-life information by dowsing maps, your body, your possessions, pictures and photographs.

- **Astrology:** Your birth chart holds past-life information in your north and south nodes, and your retrograde planets.

- **Crystals:** Holding crystals or carrying them with you will enhance any meditation. There are specific crystals that will help you to access a spiritual view of your reincarnation journey, heal past-life wounds, explore past lives in other worlds and on other planets, and discover your past lives through the Akashic Records.

- **Dreams:** Dreams set in historical times are usually about past lives. You can find out more about them by keeping a dream journal, going back into the dream, asking for a new dream to give you clear answers, and by understanding the language of dream symbols.

- **Guided visualization:** this is a way of using symbolic imagery to help you access deeper information within yourself. The main sources are CDs, books, workshops, therapy sessions in person, or via Skype or phone.

- **Self-regression:** the three keys are intention, relaxation and trust. When you're ready, you can choose one of three vehicles to take you on your journey.

Discovering that you had past lives is like suddenly inheriting an enormous mansion. The first wing you explore is all about finding out what kind of past lives you had. The wing that lies beyond that is about how to use that information to improve your life now.

The next section in this book will take you into that new wing – how to find and use the many gifts that your past lives have in store for you.

Part II

THE BENEFITS
OF PAST-LIFE
AWARENESS

*'It's not the events of our lives that shape us,
but our beliefs about what those events mean.'*
TONY ROBBINS

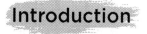

Introduction

Who am I? Where did I come from? Why am I here? Most people wonder about these things at some point in their lives. With past-life knowledge, we can access for ourselves the positive and life-affirming answers to those questions.

Who am I?

Just accepting that we had past lives immediately expands our sense of who we really are. It becomes clear that our real identity is not the everyday self that the world sees.

The characters that we become in our different lives are like outfits of clothing. At the end of every life we discard them, and take on another when we begin a new life. As we continue along our soul journey, we inhabit many different personalities. But our real identity is the inner spirit that travels from life to life. Seeing ourselves in this way transforms our entire outlook on life. We lose the fears, illusions and anxieties that go with identifying too closely with the ego self.

Past-life awareness also helps us to avoid becoming inflated by successful lives or disempowered by humble ones. In the words of Buddha, 'Who toiled a slave may come anew a prince, for gentle worthiness and merit won. Who ruled a king may wander Earth in rags, for things done and undone.'

Knowing that our current self is part of a much larger, benign and supportive structure provides a deep sense of security. Yearning to belong to a bigger meaningful whole, many people blindly seek that in the outside world. But when we know who we really are, that old neediness withers away like an uprooted weed.

Where did I come from?

In one way, we come from the many places we've been to on our long reincarnation journey. The memories we gained there will always be part of us. But those places are not our true home. Our true home is in the spirit realm. This has been confirmed by the many memories that people have of the between-life worlds.

'The Earth plane is a training school, to which we return lifetime after lifetime, each of us bearing our own spiritual satchel of inclinations, wisdom and experience garnered from previous lives,' wrote past-life researcher Joe Fisher.

We go back to the spiritual world between every life to rest, recover and enjoy life at home again. When we're ready to return to the school of earthly lives, wise guides will help us to decide what sort of life to take on next.

They also help us to clarify the purpose of our next

incarnation. When we return, we carry that knowledge deep in our hearts. Even if we're not fully conscious of it, that inner knowing will guide us through our lives.

Why am I here?

Knowing about reincarnation automatically gives meaning to life. It becomes clear that even if we don't fully understand it, there is a higher purpose to our sojourn on this plane.

There are also many individual reasons for coming here, such as:

- To mature and develop along our spiritual path.

- To heal a relationship.

- To strengthen ourselves in weak areas.

- To continue learning or studying a favourite skill or subject.

- To forgive ourselves and others.

- To continue or complete what we began in an earlier life.

- To prepare for long-term aims that may still be far in the distance.

Past-life knowledge shows us the themes and stories that we may have been exploring for many lifetimes. This helps to clarify our purpose in this life. We can then begin to answer the age-old question: why am I here?

The personal benefits of past-life awareness

Apart from making our lives richer and more interesting,

understanding past lives also brings us specific benefits.

First, it gives meaning to our lives, and a sense of higher purpose. Being cut off from this understanding is the root cause of many psychological problems. The great psychoanalyst and psychiatrist Dr Carl Jung said, 'How often have I heard a patient exclaim, "If only I knew that my life had some meaning and purpose, then there would be no silly story about my nerves!"'

When we know about past lives, it becomes impossible to fear death in the old way again. Fear of death feeds all kinds of other fears, phobias and neuroses. When that's gone, it releases us from a wide range of troublesome issues that can hamper our lives in so many ways.

'The unresolved trauma of death is a primary cause of behavioural disorders,' said past-life therapist Dr Morris Netherton. 'Most of the problems I encounter have their source in past-life deaths. When the impact of these deaths is erased, many disorders simply evaporate.'

Studies have been conducted about the healing effects of belief in reincarnation on post-traumatic stress disorder. The evidence shows that people who believe in rebirth have more resilience. When life knocks them down, they soon bounce back again.

Reincarnation also means that there is a higher form of justice. According to the law of karma, we all reap what we sow. This means that life isn't as unfair as it seems to be. Everyone's deeds, both good and bad, catch up with them in the end across their many lives.

Knowing how past-life experiences can still affect us helps us to deal with them. When we become conscious of old wounds, they lose their power over us.

'Those who cannot remember the past are condemned to repeat it', said the philosopher George Santayana. We release ourselves from the past by first becoming aware of its effects. We can then untie any knots that have been holding us back. This frees us to move forward into a better future.

Seeing the higher purpose behind an experience is one of the best ways to heal its negative effects. Jung said we reduce suffering by finding the meaning in a difficult event.

Past-life awareness shows us the inner meaning of our experiences. This helps us to transcend and transform their effects. When we understand the 'lesson' of an event, we stop seeing ourselves as baffled victims of life, and the old symptoms melt away.

Past-life knowledge also benefits many important areas of our lives, such as health, relationships, prosperity and self-worth.

Benefits to the world

Belief in reincarnation is not only beneficial to us as individuals, it also has the potential to sow the seeds of hugely positive future effects for the world in general.

More tolerance

Understanding how rebirth works leads people to identify less narrowly with their gender, social class and nationality. In different lives, we've all been both male and female. We've lived in many different countries. We've sometimes been wealthy and sometimes poor. Knowing this makes it difficult for people to pride themselves too much on the circumstances they were born into this time. That kind of arrogance becomes much trickier with the knowledge that in a future life the tables could so easily be turned.

As a result, there could be less temptation to despise, mistreat or oppress others who don't currently enjoy the same advantages. In this way, reincarnation beliefs can help to starve the strangling weeds of elitism, sexism and racism in our society.

The Dalai Lama said: 'The belief in rebirth should engender a universal love because all living things and creatures, in the course of their numberless lives and our own, have been our beloved parents, children, brothers, sisters, friends.'

More peace

As well as bringing more love, tolerance and understanding to the world, a general acceptance of reincarnation could help to foster world peace.

Successful entrepreneur Henry Ford once remarked, 'The discovery of reincarnation put my mind at ease. I would like to communicate to others the calmness that the long view of life gives to us.'

When we are at peace with life and ourselves, we are at peace with the world. If the majority of people felt like that, it would change the way the world operates.

Wars always have their overt rationales and justifications, but the hidden emotional drive behind many conflicts is a primitive fear of the enemy for being so 'other'. When more people realize that we've all had lives in a wide range of diverse cultures, it will be much harder to fear and hate people for being different.

With this underlying philosophy, all kinds of potential conflicts could be more easily defused before they even start. Peace might then start to replace war as the favourite way to solve problems.

Less materialism

Belief in rebirth brings with it a more spiritual view of life. This has great potential to weaken the dominance of materialism – firstly in individual lives, then in society as a whole. New, more spiritually aware, priorities could then emerge to reshape our world and way of life. This too would help to create a more unified, peaceful and tolerant world.

Valuing each life

Perhaps the greatest benefit to the world that reincarnation beliefs can bring is the affirmation of individual self-worth. The Hindu religion compares our lives to a silver string of pearls, called the Sutratma. The thread is the soul, and each life is a pearl of priceless worth. This philosophy affirms the innate value of each life, no matter how humble.

Because every life plays a part in our story, they are all important. They all have purpose and meaning. Seeing life in this way nurtures the deepest roots of self-worth. With those roots secure, it becomes much easier to flower. And when every flower is valued, a happier and more loving world becomes possible.

Chapter 11

Health

One of the most noticeable benefits of past-life knowledge is how it can improve our health. The mind affects the body all the time. Many people now think that there is a psycho-spiritual dimension to every ailment. Past lives, in particular, can have a direct influence on our physical wellbeing. Understanding how this works is one of the biggest health breakthroughs in recent history. It means that we can alleviate, and even completely heal, a wide range of physical problems by understanding the emotional reason behind them. Those reasons usually come from a past-life experience.

As with all important breakthroughs, this was simmering under the surface but resisted for a long time. In the nineteenth century, King Ferdinand of Naples ordered Lafontaine, a Swiss hypnotist, to leave Naples unless 'he made no more blind people see nor deaf ones hear'.

When he heard about this, Pope Pius IX commented. 'Well, Monsieur Lafontaine, let us hope that, for the good of humanity, hypnotism may soon be generally employed.'

Over a hundred years later, the seed of that hope is now flowering. It was tended and watered by the pioneers who discovered how past lives affect our health.

Some key game-changers

Edgar Cayce, the great psychic healer, diagnosed many physical issues as having a past-life cause. In one of his readings, he said that a woman had beautiful hands because of lives spent in selfless service to others.

On another occasion he told a deaf person not to shut his ears again to those who asked for help. That past-life deed was the cause of his deafness in this life.

In another diagnosis, Cayce stated that a woman had been born disfigured because she'd persecuted others during a life in imperial Rome. In her lives since then she'd achieved great spiritual development. Her physical problems in this life were the last bit of karma she had to deal with around that issue. All she needed to do was accept it, and after this life she'd start incarnating on higher planes.

The woman said that in childhood she'd been fascinated by anything to do with ancient Rome. After this reading she worked on overcoming her difficulties with 'willpower, patience and prayer'. In this way she completely healed herself – not just physically, but spiritually and emotionally as well.

Past-life therapist **Dr Morris Netherton** didn't believe in reincarnation to start with. He went for counselling because of feelings of inadequacy made worse by a chronic bleeding stomach ulcer. As he talked about all the pain he was in, a past-life memory came up. He found himself in a nineteenth-century Mexican prison for the criminally insane. A guard had kicked him in the stomach in the exact spot where his ulcer had developed in this life.

He had been in that prison because his wife had committed him as mentally unsound. She did this so that she could seize his land. With a shock, he realized she was also his current wife. She had become his wife again to make up for how she'd treated him in their former life together.

That night, he took her out for dinner. When he told her about this, he said 'She passed out in her mashed potatoes.'

After that, the pain of his ulcer never returned. He went on to get a doctorate in psychology, and became a leading light in the field of past-life therapy. In his writings he described many cases in which finding the past-life cause helped to cure serious physical complaints such as epilepsy, migraine and incipient cancer.

Psychiatrist **Dr Arthur Guirdham** was also sceptical about past lives at first. But he later declared 'There is no disease known to man the cause of which is entirely determined in what is called his own lifetime.'

Past-life researcher and author **Dr Helen Wambach** regressed a woman who was having occasional seizures. There was no medical reason for them and no attempts to cure them had worked. When they happened, the woman said it felt like 'Going a million miles an hour'.

In the regression she went back to a life in sixteenth-century France. She'd been to visit a sick child. When the infant later died, the villagers said she'd killed it with witchcraft. In a torchlit procession, they carried her to the cliffs. Then they threw her over them to her death. The seizures were her body's memory of the terror of hurtling to the ground below. After the regression, her seizures stopped and never returned.

Hypnotherapist **Dr Michael Pollack** had a lower-back pain that grew steadily worse over the years. In his article *Have We Really Lived Before?* he said he'd experienced at least three past lives in which he'd been killed by a knife or a spear in his back. Once he knew the cause of the pain, his back problem disappeared.

Professor Ian Stevenson described a case in Sri Lanka of a boy who'd been born with a deformed right breast and arm. His right hand couldn't hold anything.

When he was about three years old, his mother said he started muttering to himself in a dark, solitary way. As she listened in, it became clear that he thought his arm was deformed because he'd murdered his wife in a past life.

The boy mentioned a number of verifiable details about that life – and it all checked out. He turned out to be the reincarnation of his father's brother. That man had been executed in 1928 for the murder of his wife. His father said the boy had always reminded him of his late brother. From then on, both parents did everything they could to help and heal their child.

Dr Roger Woolger said 'The body and its various aches, pains and dysfunctions is a living psychic history book when read correctly.' He found that the body as a whole, as well as any part of the body, can carry the imprints of past-life shocks. These can come out in all kinds of weaknesses or disabilities.

He recommended the following healing methods:

- Bodywork, such as massage. This relieves both physical and emotional pain, especially when focused on the neck, the back and the head.

- Deep breathing. See the in-breath cleansing the body of all past issues; use each out-breath to release and let go of old wounds.

- The use of healing magnets to draw old emotional pain out of the body.

- Acupuncture or acupressure to clear the inner meridians, which get clogged up by long-standing emotional issues. The blockages then create health problems.

The main problems

In my experience, the most common and widespread past-life effects on health are:

1. Weight and eating disorders
2. Skin problems
3. Breathing difficulties.

1. Weight

In her extensive past-life researches Dr Helen Wambach found that until the sixteenth century, people lived mostly on gruel, roots and berries, fruits from trees and the occasional, small wild animal.

They had to scavenge for most of these things themselves. None of it was abundantly available, especially in bad seasons. So for the majority of people, hunger and starvation were always waiting in the wings, ever ready to strike.

Many people have experienced this kind of past life. Being reborn into a world that's full of cheap and satisfying food would be like one of their wildest dreams come true. Survival is our strongest instinct. The basic compulsion for a lot of people would be to have as much of this food as possible before it all goes away again.

Dr Edith Fiore found that practically all her patients who were overweight by more than 4.5kg (10lbs) had been through a lifetime in which they either starved to death or suffered long periods of food deprivation.

The last in line

One of my clients, Leila, came for a regression about the problems she was having with losing weight. She went back to a past life in ancient Egypt, when she was a little girl in a large family. In times of famine or shortage the most important members of the family were fed first. She was always at the end of the queue. As a result she died of malnutrition at a young age.

That life created an unconscious fear of famine. This drove her to eat as much as possible when food was available. When Leila realized where the problem had come from, it lost its hold on her.

Fast food and the monk

Even when food deprivation is voluntary, it can have a similar effect in later lives. When Peter came for a regression he went back to a life in a monastery near London. He said his father in that life could remember the coming of William the Conqueror.

As a monk, he was very aware of the need to be humble. This meant always looking down, hardly talking and eating as little as possible. He believed in it all – but felt that the monastery applied it too harshly.

In later years, an epidemic killed many of the monks. When that happened, the old strict ways softened. The monks were allowed to talk to each other more. Life in the monastery became gentler.

Then Peter also fell ill. As he lay dying, he saw with joy his mother coming to take him to the higher worlds. He said it was a relief to leave that life behind.

Afterwards he told me that he was now the manager of a fast-food outlet. He could eat whatever he wanted there, and had overdone it. Now on a diet, he said he'd lost four stone, with 'four more to go'.

The regression showed him that gorging on fast food had been his way of making up for the strict monastic life. With the help of this knowledge he lost even more weight, and soon moved on to a better job.

Refusing to eat

Sometimes food issues from past lives can show up in more troubled ways than simply overeating. For example, Dr Bruce Goldberg wrote about a woman who had anorexia nervosa because she was punishing herself for a past life when she'd been a fat and selfish man.

'Eating disorders such as anorexia nervosa and bulimia often reveal old stories of starvation due to crop failure, famine or disease', wrote Dr Roger Woolger, adding that 'more and more cases of starvation from World War Two, especially in concentration camps, are now surfacing from the unconscious in contemporary cases of anorexia and other eating disorders.'

The brave nun

Those words turned out to be prophetically true in Venetia's case. She'd always been interested in having a past-life regression. So for a birthday treat her husband arranged for her to come and see me.

She had a bubbly personality and was slightly plump. That turned out to be a good sign. In her teens she'd become bulimic but was now on medication to keep the bulimia under control.

In her regression she went back to a church. It was wartime. She was a nun, trying to hide a group of terrified people. To keep them safe, she was desperately repeating her rosary. But Nazi soldiers suddenly broke in and took them all away. They ripped off the wimple that covered her hair. Then they threw her into a concentration camp for having tried to hide the others.

The only food there was very thin soup – almost water – and stale bread. Close to starving, she had vivid memories of stuffing the bread into her mouth as fast as possible. Because of the conditions there she didn't survive for long. Afterwards she said the way she'd gobbled the bread while in the concentration camp reminded her of her bulimic episodes. At those times, she'd eat as much as possible and then throw it all up.

As a nun in that life she'd felt guilty and ashamed about eating at all. Others in the camp needed that food. She'd blamed herself for not being above such 'selfish' behaviour.

After the regression Venetia realized that her experience as the nun had given her needless guilt about eating. This was the unconscious cause of her bulimia. Now that she understood its underlying dynamics, it would be even easier to leave behind.

In an interesting postscript, she told me that some time before she'd seen some photographs in a newspaper of concentration-camp victims from the Second World War. At the time, she'd had a strong feeling that she knew one of the men in the photographs. After her regression, she realized that she really had *recognized someone from the concentration camp.*

Of course, not every eating disorder or weight problem may stem from such dramatic causes. A life of just scratching and scrounging for bits of food can have its effects as well. But when we understand the causes of previously unconscious behaviour, it puts us, rather than our syndromes, in charge. We can then shake off those effects and move ahead in a more conscious and healthier way.

2. Skin problems

The skin is especially sensitive to our emotions. It can express unconscious fears, anger or guilt with symptoms like acne, warts or rashes.

Persistent conditions, such as eczema or psoriasis, may come from:

1. Having been burned or killed by fire

2. Having been attacked, tortured or killed by poison or acid

3. Fatal diseases with skin eruptions, such as smallpox or the plague.

The confession

In her regression Molly went back to a life as a young man in a tribal society. He was newly wed and they had a young baby. He'd just returned home after a time away. His wife was delighted to see him again. But there was something bad he had to tell her. He couldn't bring himself to do that. To avoid it, he kept busy feeding the chickens.

In the end he went to consult the village elder. There he confessed that in an argument, he'd killed a man from another village. He felt deeply sorry about it. The elder said he'd have to pay the full price because the other village would insist on it.

The price was death by fire. He accepted his fate. He went home to tell his wife and they wept together.

After a while he asked for the execution to go ahead soon, as he couldn't bear the wait. He was overwhelmed with guilt about having ruined so many lives and for having thrown his own young life away.

When they led him to the fire he went willingly. But he lacked the final courage to walk into it by himself. They had to push him. He felt the agonizing flames licking around his feet and ankles – and then remembered no more.

After the regression, sipping a restorative cup of tea, Molly showed me the psoriasis she'd always had on her feet and ankles. It looked just like the burns from a fire. She said when she had been at school she'd had some bizarre reactions to the fire drill. It had often sent her into a panic. This memory explained why she feared even the suggestion of fire.

Molly left feeling optimistic that she was well on her way to resolving her issues and curing her psoriasis.

3. Breathing problems

In one of his talks, Dr Roger Woolger said that when a traumatic event occurs in our life, we take in a big gasp – and psychologically never let it out again. From then on, through future lives, this holds us in a stasis of fear until we can find a way to release ourselves from that stuck moment.

This is why deep breathing exercises can do so much to heal emotional issues. Everyone who has a regression starts by breathing slowly and deeply, which is an important part of the whole process.

Persistent coughing, shortness of breath and asthma are the three most common ways past-life experiences can affect the breath. Deaths by drowning, smothering, asphyxiation, gassing or strangulation are the main culprits. Experiences of emotional suffocation can also cause these conditions.

Terror in the mist

Colleen came for a regression because of a mild but persistent asthma problem. She told me that she already knew of two possible past-life causes for it.

She'd accessed the first one at a workshop a few years earlier. It was a mostly happy life in the sixteenth century, but she'd contracted tuberculosis and died young.

The other possibility came from a vivid dream she'd had of being a Cornish fisherman. He had died with something covering his face, so that he couldn't breathe.

The third big clue came when she went into a museum and saw a display that produced a lot of mist as one of its effects. That sent her into a panic, as she felt terrified she was about to die.

In the regression we did she didn't go back to any of those lives – perhaps it would have been too traumatic. Instead, she accessed a memory that gave her an important message about staying positive and trusting in life. That memory is described in more detail in Chapter 14 (see page 185).

In the second part of her regression, she asked a spirit guide about her asthma problem. He said it came from a deep-seated fear that she needed to release – the fear of death. He told her that she could never die and her spirit will always live on. As he continued reassuring her about this, she let out some huge sighs of relief. I felt it was a positive sign that healing was already under way.

The spirit guide also said that breathing in the sea air would help to cure her asthma, because it had come mainly from the life as a fisherman. She'd panicked about the mist in the museum because mist had caused her boat to crash onto rocks and turn over, leading to her death in that life. She was partly suffocated by the sail before she drowned. Her asthma was her body's way of still trying to gasp for air.

Her guide said that taking deep breaths of sea air – especially in misty conditions – would be especially healing for her. It would finally lay those fears to rest.

Afterwards she told me that she'd felt drawn to the sea for a while now. Lately she'd been thinking about moving to the coast. This session confirmed her decision. She left in an optimistic mood, looking forward to the future.

The chakras

The spirit self transmits past-life effects to the body through the chakras, which are invisible energy centres in the body, aligned with the major glands. The glands respond to the chakras by secreting enzymes. These are chemical messengers that have a huge influence on our mental, emotional and physical lives.

'Chakra' is a Sanskrit word, meaning 'wheel' or 'vortex'. The chakras are also often likened to the petals of a flower, which can be open or closed. When the petals are closed, the chakra is inactive. Negative past-life experiences can cause a particular chakra to weaken or close down. For example, the heart chakra may be closed because of hurtful experiences in a former lifetime.

When it's open, the energies of the chakra can flower and flow freely. The ancient Indian symbol of the thousand-petalled lotus represents the higher consciousness that comes with a fully opened chakra system.

Healing the past-life issues that are holding us back is one of the most effective ways to transform our lives. The chakras are like the engine room of all our issues. This is why a regular chakra-clearing, balancing and strengthening exercise (*see page 150*) can make a huge difference to our health and wellbeing.

Each chakra has its own colour. The clearer and brighter this colour, the healthier the chakra. Working with colour healing is a powerful therapy on its own – and it's even more effective when combined with a chakra-clearing exercise.

The seven main chakras

1. Root/base chakra
Location: at the base of the spine
Colour: red
Affects: adrenalin glands
Influences: physical energy; actions; survival; security

2. Sacral chakra
Location: about 7.5cm (3in) below the navel
Colour: orange
Affects: reproductive glands
Influences: creativity; sexuality; emotional drives and desires

3. Solar plexus chakra
Location: just above the navel
Colour: yellow
Affects: pancreas
Influences: mental activity; willpower

4. Heart chakra
Location: heart area
Colour: green
Affects: thymus gland
Influences: higher emotions, such as love, kindness and joy

5. Throat chakra
Location: throat area
Colour: blue
Affects: thyroid gland
Influences: communication – both speaking and hearing

6. Brow/third-eye chakra
Location: forehead
Colour: violet
Affects: pineal gland
Influences: second sight; visions; spiritual views

7. Crown chakra
Location: top of the head
Colour: white
Affects: pituitary gland
Influences: connections to higher consciousness

Exercise: Clearing your chakras

Get into a relaxed and comfortable state, when you won't be interrupted. Let go of all outside concerns. Breathe slowly and deeply. Imagine all your muscles softening and melting.

Red
Imagine yourself completely surrounded with a warm, clear shade of red. The colour fills your whole body. It releases tensions, bringing you energy, vitality and a deep sense of security.

Visualize a red flower becoming brighter and more open every time you do this exercise.

Orange

See the red now gradually change to a beautiful warm orange colour. It fills you up and completely surrounds you.

This colour brings a healthy balance to your emotional life, especially your creativity and sexuality.

Envision an orange flower becoming brighter and more open every time you do this exercise.

Yellow

Imagine the orange colour now smoothly changing to a beautiful warm shade of golden yellow, like the rays of the sun. It surrounds you and fills you up.

This colour brings a healthy balance to your mental activities and the use of your willpower.

Visualize a yellow flower becoming brighter and more open every time you do this exercise.

Green

Watch as the yellow now slowly changes to a warm shade of green – the colour of nature and fresh growth. It surrounds you and fills you up with the energies of love and joy.

Envision a green flower becoming brighter and more open every time you do this exercise.

Blue

See the green now softly change to a beautiful shade of warm blue, like the sky on a sunny day. It surrounds you and fills you up with a calm sense of openness.

You can speak out in safety and clarity. You are open to hear all the good things that life can teach you.

Imagine a blue flower becoming brighter and more open every time you do this exercise.

Violet

Watch as the blue colour now gradually changes to a beautiful and vibrant shade of violet, like the colour of deep twilight.

This surrounds you and fills you up, giving energy to your third eye, your second sight and your ability to see beyond physicality.

Envision a violet flower becoming brighter and more open every time you do this exercise.

White

Imagine the violet now smoothly changing to a clear white light, with some sparkles of gold in it. This light surrounds you and fills you up.

It brings you a clear connection to the guidance of higher consciousness and your soul's purpose for this life.

See a white flower becoming brighter and more open every time you do this exercise.

The rainbow

Now envision the white joined by all the other colours – violet, blue, green, yellow, orange and red – to create a rainbow energy.

The warm, clear rainbow completely fills and surrounds you, bringing healing and peace to all aspects of your being – physical, emotional, mental and spiritual.

You can do this exercise as often as you wish. The more you do it, the more it will benefit you.

The particular kinds of flowers you see may have personal significance for you. They may also give you clues about past-life experiences in the area they represent.

Over time, you may notice the flowers that you visualize getting clearer and brighter. It means that your chakras are becoming open and energized. This will help to heal a wide range of past-life issues, and have a positive impact on your health at every level of your being.

SUMMARY

Over the last century, major breakthroughs have taken place in understanding how much our minds and emotions affect our bodies.

- Past-life experiences have emerged as one of the most important influences on our health.

- For decades now, therapists and psychologists have found that understanding the past-life cause can help, and even completely cure, a wide range of physical problems.

- As well as regression, there are also exercises, treatments, therapies and visualizations that will do much to heal a physical problem caused by a past-life experience. Hopefully one day this kind of holistic healing will be so widespread that it will raise the general standard of health for everyone.

Chapter 12

Abundance

Like good health, enjoying a comfortable standard of living is our natural state. We take these things for granted when we have them because they are our birthright. When people have money problems it's often because of past-life issues. Understanding how that works gives us the key to free ourselves from those difficulties.

The first step is to realize that although it may seem so, it's not really the past-life experiences that affect us. It's the attitudes that we adopt as a result of our experiences. Those beliefs become a semi-permanent part of our psyche. From then on they operate from the subconscious to create our lives and experiences – for better or for worse. For example, poverty often comes from a deep-seated belief that having money is not spiritual. But is this really true? It's like saying that air is bad because bad people breathe it. Money is just a resource. It really is possible to be spiritual and well off at the same time.

When it's in the right hands money can do a lot of good in the world. Unfortunately most of the people who'd use money in constructive, benevolent ways are busy keeping themselves poor because they believe this is the best way to be spiritual.

The three main past-life reasons that cause people to block the flow of abundance into their lives are: disillusion, religious beliefs and fears.

Disillusion

A wealthy past life can be a two-edged sword. It's like having power – the test is learning how to handle it. For those who've never experienced a wealthy life before, some of the first pitfalls are the temptations to be selfish, greedy or obsessive about it.

At the end of every life we look back and review how we did. Although there are kindly guides to help us, the harshest judgements we'll ever experience come from ourselves.

The first disillusionment

People who are ashamed of the way they handled wealth often decide that they don't deserve to have it again. Disillusioned about themselves, they feel that they must now have lives of poverty and struggle. However, that solution also has its pitfalls.

This is because when we've condemned ourselves, we are quick to condemn others. When we can forgive ourselves, we can also forgive others. Judgement and punishment is not the best path to take – even if we think we deserve it.

It helps to see past-life mistakes as a natural part of the soul journey on this plane. We have all come here to learn and grow. It's a tough school, and everyone stumbles and falls sometimes. The best way to get up and move forward again is to understand the real point of the lesson. Money issues are often about learning how to accept the natural abundance of life with grace, gratitude and good will.

Forgiving ourselves for past mistakes and taking a positive view about money will clear old blockages and allow our natural abundance to flow freely again.

The other disillusionment

This is with money itself – usually because it didn't solve the problems we thought it would. At the end of that kind of life, people often decide that money isn't worth having because it wasn't the magic wand they expected it to be.

Then the next time they incarnate, they wonder why they live on the poor side of town and have problems paying their bills. At that point it becomes clear that poverty doesn't solve any problems either – and may create even more. The best ladder out of that pit is a new, more positive way of thinking about money.

The sad inheritance

Dennis came for a regression to see if he could find out why he never had any money, however hard he worked. He went back to a past life in an English manor house. It had leaded windows, with medieval-looking banners and tapestries on the walls.

He was a boy of about 14 – and feeling very alone. His parents had gone. He never found out exactly why.

He thought they'd displeased the king, and had been taken away because of that.

As the oldest boy, he inherited the mansion. But he felt cut off from everyone around him. It seemed to him that wealth had brought him nothing but misery and loneliness. He grew to hate it because of that.

Dennis had been carrying this dark experience unhealed within him ever since. In the second part of the session, I suggested that he visualize a place of healing where he could receive spiritual help about this. He said there were beings of light there. They swirled around him, murmuring soft words.

He couldn't make out what they were saying, but knew it was healing in some way. As they did that, he began to realize that he'd decided to cut himself off from having money because he feared a repeat of that lonely medieval life.

When it was time to leave the place of healing, one of the light beings gave him a beautiful carved box. It had a large gold coin inside. This was a symbol of the abundance that he'd been denying himself – and which was now being restored.

Religious beliefs

For the last two thousand years and more, people who wanted to follow a serious spiritual path usually joined a dedicated community. Once there, they had few personal possessions, but their basic needs were covered.

At the beginning of the Piscean Age, over 2,000 years ago, the Judeo-Christian ascetic sect the Essenes emerged as one of the most influential of the spiritual groups. Their whole way of life was defined by the belief that poverty is spiritual.

Ever since then, that way has been central to Christianity. It applied not only to official monasteries and nunneries, but also to heretical groups like the Gnostics and the Cathars. Compared to the challenges and responsibilities of the world outside – especially in the darker times – a cloistered life had its attractions. It may have been spartan, but it offered security, protection, fellowship and a sense of higher purpose.

Many people on a spiritual path today have spent at least one life in this kind of community. They may have decided to go a more individual way this time. But the old ways of the cloister can still run deep within them.

Until they understand the syndrome, they may unconsciously replicate the conditions of those past lives in a kind of monastery-for-one. As a result, their basic needs will always be covered, but they won't be able to afford luxuries.

The trapped monk

Charlie came for a regression because he was curious about past-life people who might be in his life now. He went back to a life in a medieval monastery.

During that life the Abbot had treated him quite badly, but Charlie had suppressed his feelings about this.

He thought he had to put up with unfair ways out of religious duty. Apart from that, he also had nowhere else to go.

As soon as he'd remembered that life, Charlie wanted to come out of the regression. He said he needed to talk about something.

Over a cup of coffee, he told me he'd suddenly realized that history was repeating itself. He was currently working as a gardener for a widower at a big country house. This man was the reincarnation of the unpleasant Abbot of his earlier life.

Charlie said that working there wasn't as bad as it had been in the monastery, but he was still putting up with all kinds of extra, unpaid demands on his time.

'I've been ignoring my negative feelings', he said. 'I thought I should be grateful that I have a nice place to work. But I can see now that I've been replaying the old story from the monastery. And I don't have to do that any more.'

A couple of months later he told me that he'd successfully moved on to a better job, with more money and fairer conditions. He said that doing so felt weirdly frightening at first. But before long, his fear subsided and he started feeling happier than he'd been for a long time.

Life had put him back into a similar situation for a good reason. It was so that he could finally give that story a happy ending. At the same time, he was also able to release other monastic restrictions that had been holding him back – especially the belief that it's unspiritual to earn money.

'My inner monk finally realized it was OK to make money,' he said. 'And it feels great!'

Fears

Because money can be such an emotionally charged issue, it can give fear all kinds of excuses to move into our psyche. Those fears will then steer us onto paths that seem safe, but may not be the best paths to take. For example, we may decide that being well off is just too dangerous. In past lives, it may have attracted jealousy and resentment. It might even have sparked off personal attacks ranging from whispered spite to outright murder.

After a life like that, it seems safer to avoid having money altogether. But as Beverly found in her regression, this is not the answer.

The revolution

'I'm a young woman. I've got a big white wig on. I'm wearing a beautiful dress. It's got pearls on it. I have a diamond necklace and bracelets.

'I seem to be preparing for a party. I'm lighting candles and feeling happy and excited. Life is full of fun.'

After a long pause, Beverly described a very different scene. She was running somewhere. Her clothes were dirty. She'd lost everything. She knew her pursuers were about to catch her. She stumbled and fell face down on the ground. After that the memory ended.

We moved on to the next part of the session. She was able to access her inner guidance, and learned that this life had taken place during the French Revolution. In that life she was guillotined for having been wealthy. As a result, she became afraid ever to have money again. On top of that, she was always careful not to look well-off in any way.

When we discussed her next steps, she decided to start by wearing things that she'd never dared to before. She used to worry that they would attract the wrong kind of attention – but realized now that this was a needless fear.

I knew exactly what she meant, because as I mentioned in the main Introduction (see page 3), my past life in the French Revolution had affected me in a similar way.

As Beverley and I discussed those experiences, it was strange to think that here were two people who'd been guillotined – now chatting about it in safety and comfort.

We never die. And we can recover from anything that life may throw at us. Most of the long-term damage comes from the negative beliefs that we have formed because of those experiences.

The best way to a happy life is to become aware of those effects – and then let them go. This is why knowing about past lives is so beneficial. Understanding where our blockages come from makes it easy to clear them away. We can then benefit from positive attitudes about everything – including money, wealth and abundance in all its forms.

Exercise: Enhancing your abundance

There are other things you can do that will move the process along. The following 12 techniques will all help to increase your abundance and transform your life.

❖ Decide you are not a victim, and that you have the power to change your life.

❖ Understand the past-life cause of a money problem.

❖ Rethink your beliefs about money.

❖ Have imaginary talks with your past selves about your new beliefs.

❖ Forgive yourself and others for past-life mistakes.

❖ Take a positive, higher view of your reincarnation journey.

❖ Decide that you deserve abundance in your life.

❖ Count your blessings – from the biggest to the smallest.

❖ Focus on how money is coming to you and see the flow increasing.

❖ Visualize how you'd live with unlimited abundance.

❖ Imagine the many different ways that you could benefit others if you had greater abundance.

❖ Say affirmations, such as 'I live in a safe, benign and abundant universe.

SUMMARY

The ideal way of life is to have whatever material resources we need to be happy and comfortable, without sacrificing our inner values. Some of the main blocks that stop us achieving this are the negative conclusions we've come to because of past-life experiences.

Abundance issues can affect us in three main ways:

- Disillusionment: about how we mishandled wealth in a past life, and about how money wasn't the answer to everything.

- Religious beliefs: The belief that poverty is spiritual.

- Fears: If past-life wealth brought on envy and/or attacks from others, all kinds of unconscious fears and blockages about money can be created in subsequent lives.

Chapter 13

Relationships

Our important relationships are like long-running sagas. They can take lifetimes to unfold. What we see of them in our current lives is only one episode. Just knowing that alters how we relate to people. It gives us a higher, more philosophical view of the relationship. This rubs off on others, leading to greater peace and understanding all round.

When we delve into the past-life roots of a particular relationship, we can find the source of any problem it might be going through. We can then find a positive resolution much quicker than if we'd stayed unconscious of how the issue began.

Along the way, it often becomes clear that the tangle was just a temporary issue. Once it's smoothed out, we can get back to the happy relationship we had with that person – perhaps lifetimes ago.

As Dr Morris Netherton, founder of the Institute for Past Life Awareness, said, 'Past-life therapy allows you to stop doing things to people because you have to, and to start doing things with people because you want to.'

Positive past-life connections

Many people come into our lives for positive past-life reasons. We often recognize them the moment we meet. Although we've never seen them in this life before, we intuitively feel that we know them. There may also be a strong sense of destiny about the meeting.

When I was at a talk one evening, during the interval I got chatting with one of the women there. She told me that she'd met a man a little while ago – and had immediately known that they'd been close in a past life.

She said that as they'd made small talk, memories from that life had started welling up into her mind. He'd been shot in the hip by an arrow. She was tending to the wound. She sensed that he still had problems in that area.

Tentatively, she'd asked him if this was the case. Surprised by her question, he'd said she was right. He'd had problems in that area, which the doctors hadn't been able to fix.

As they talked it over, it became clear that their meeting was somehow fated. She said later on that their meeting had turned out to be the beginning of a new chapter for them. It was the continuation of a happy relationship that had been strong for hundreds of years.

The Romany soulmate
. . . .

Julie wasn't born into a Romany family, but in childhood she had recurring dreams about colourful gypsy caravans. While growing up, she never had any contact with that kind of world. She certainly never had any training in their ways. But by her twelfth year she knew how to tell fortunes with mirrors and cards. She became a sensation among her friends, because she could see into their futures – and her forecasts came true.

Children are still close to their former lives. Their dreams of other cultures give us good clues about those lives. Unexpected skills that come up are even bigger signs. On looking back, it's now obvious that Julie had a past life as a Romany seer. But it wasn't clear at the time – least of all to Julie herself.

So as she grew up, she left those ways behind. She married a successful and wealthy businessman. But after a few years of that lifestyle, she sank into a depression. She fell seriously ill, and ended up in hospital.

This kind of healing crisis occasionally happens when we're at an important crossroads in life. At times of major change, this is how life sometimes moves us on.

While in hospital, Julie realized that her chosen lifestyle wasn't right for her. It was time to rethink everything.

Once she'd recovered, she started looking for a new direction in life. She began by going to the Romany clairvoyant, Lee Petulengro.

He gave her so many accurate details about her life that she was convinced he was genuinely psychic. Among other things, he told her that she had 'everything, but nothing of any real value'. He saw that she was married with a son, and that she wanted to walk away and start again – with nothing if necessary.

His final prediction was that she would find her real soulmate, marry him and have a daughter. He said she'd already met this man. Julie said she had an uncanny feeling it was Lee himself. But she dismissed that as just a fantasy.

Sometime later, a friend asked Julie to take her to Lee for a reading. While that was going on, Julie waited outside in the car. When her friend came out, she produced a red rose. It was from Lee to Julie. He'd had a feeling she'd be around that day. When she went inside to thank him, he asked her out for lunch. From then on, they knew they were destined to be together.

As their relationship unfolded, Lee could tell that Julie had psychic skills. He encouraged her to develop them and become his equal partner. To the surprise of both of them, she found that she instantly knew the meaning of many of the Romany words Lee used. Until then, she'd never heard or read anything in that language. The only way she could have known those words was from a gypsy past life.

They are now both convinced that Julie was once a Romany clairvoyant – and that their relationship goes back for many lifetimes.

Brief encounters

We can have encounters with past-life connections that may be fleeting, but they are still important. These people may not be destined to be with us in this lifetime – but they can still give us a helping hand in passing.

We make these mutual arrangements in advance. In the between-life worlds, people often make a pact to help each other out at crucial times. Then back on Earth, just when we need some real help, the soul connection will pop up, help us over a hurdle, and be on their way again.

The bridge to Wales

Laurie yearned to live in Wales. In Chapter 4 (see page 61) I described how she was blocked from moving there for past-life reasons. When she healed that issue, the door was open for her to move there.

But at first she couldn't figure out exactly how to do that. There were still too many practical problems, so she decided to start by having a short holiday there.

The woman who ran the lodging she'd chosen was friendly and sympathetic. Laurie said she was like a grandmother to her. It was easy to pour out how much she wanted to move to Wales, but didn't know where to start.

With perfect synchronicity, this grandmotherly woman was about to advertise for a temporary live-in helper. On hearing about Laurie's dilemma, she offered her the job – and Laurie happily accepted it.

It turned out to be the perfect bridge back to Wales. Laurie felt sure that this had happened because of a past-life connection she'd had with the woman who ran the lodging. She said it had felt like being with family again, from the first day they'd met.

The destined child

Frank and Jill longed to adopt a child. But they felt worn down by all the official hurdles in their way. One day, Frank had to go and explain their case to the authorities. He did all his homework and set off armed with piles of papers.

When he sat down, the middle-aged woman behind the desk first glared at him – then stared for a moment – then seemed confused. She started shuffling through papers on her desk.

Frank launched into the little speech he'd prepared – but she held up her hand to stop him. His heart sank. Then she looked up at him and smiled. She waved a paper, saying this was all he needed. Within 10 minutes she'd given Frank the signed approval form and the meeting was over.

That was how Daisy, their beloved little girl, came into their life. Frank said both he and Jill had strange dreams about the whole thing. They're both convinced there's a past-life connection between them, their child and the woman at the office.

Resolving old problems

'Blood may be thicker than water, but judging by my results, past-life ties are a lot thicker than blood', wrote Dr Helen Wambach.

In her researches she found that 87 per cent of her regression subjects had known their current friends and families in all kinds of different relationships in their past lives. Those relationships also continue in the between-life worlds.

From all the evidence she'd gathered, Dr Wambach concluded that we all have past-life relationships that continue through many lives. We have ongoing connections not only with our loved ones, but also with people we'd rather never see again.

We reconnect with people we fear or dislike to heal the old problems. This doesn't mean accepting bad behaviour – sometimes it's just the opposite. A negative past-life connection may keep coming back until we finally stand up for ourselves.

Facing the bully

In her regression, Violetta saw a big white house, which felt like somewhere in South America. She was working there for a despotic old woman who used to make her cry with fear.

This woman was now her current mother-in-law. Violetta and her husband were living in her house for financial reasons. And she was treating Violetta in the same abusive way.

So we did an exercise in which Violetta went back into that past life to stand up to the old woman. Despite her terror, she handed in her resignation, packed her bags and left. It was difficult for her to do this. But when she knew she'd finally got away, she wept tears of relief.

We then moved to her current life. She created new, firm boundaries around herself. Then she politely but firmly refused to be bullied any longer.

Afterwards Violetta said she felt much less cowed by the situation. She couldn't understand why she'd been putting up with so much.

'It must have been because that past life was still making me afraid of her,' she said. 'I think when I get back, things are going to be very different!'

Forgive and let go

Sometimes past-life people come back into our lives because we can't move on until we've forgiven one another.

Lydia came for a regression because she said her inner guidance had told her there was something from the past that she had to put right, and she'd been led to me. She guessed that the regression would show her something that would be tough to take. So at first it was hard for her to access any clear memories. But she kept going, and I admired her tenacity and courage.

Eventually she went back to a Native American life. There was a bitter rivalry going on between herself and another woman over a man. Some sort of betrayal took place. Lydia found that too difficult to talk about. She said she felt a strong need to apologize to those people, forgive herself and finally let go of the whole thing.

When she did that, she found that the other two felt the same way. In a tearful reconciliation, the three of them forgave themselves and one another.

Afterwards Lydia said she now realized that those people were her current lodgers. This explained why there'd been so much tension between them.

She later let me know that after this regression, the problems had just melted away. When her lodgers moved on, they left in an atmosphere of peace and friendship.

Healing old insecurities

Sometimes people find themselves in relationships that are good, but which they feel insecure about because of past-life events. Unless such insecurities are addressed, they can be strong enough to shipwreck a potentially happy union.

The banishment

Janey was a happy, free spirit. Then she met an older, more conservative man. They fell in love. But she felt haunted with feelings of insecurity about him, almost bordering on dread. It was like a dark cloud over her life. So she came for a regression to find out if there was a past-life reason for this feeling.

She went back to a life in the Middle Ages. This man was her father and he was the powerful lord of a castle. Against his wishes, she'd become involved in a secret political rebellion. When he discovered this, he banished her for life. No amount of pleading could change his mind. From then on she had to make her own way in the world – and it wasn't easy.

In the second part of the session Janey's spirit guide explained why this man had come back into her life. It was not to throw her out again – instead, he was seeking forgiveness and reconciliation.

Her fear of being banished again was understandable. But he loved her deeply and wanted to make up for what he'd done. If she focused on the love they shared, all would be well.

I next heard from Janey about six months later. Her dark cloud had gone. She and her partner were happy together. She said she felt more secure now than at any other time in her life before.

The kidnap

Lynette married a man who gave her everything her heart could desire. But she was driving the relationship onto the rocks with her unnecessary possessiveness, jealousy and paranoia.

She came for a regression because she couldn't understand why she was like that. She feared that one day her husband's patience would finally wear thin, and she'd be on her own again.

In the regression she saw a bleak city street. A man was pulling a four-year-old girl along. He was a bit rough and impatient with her and she was crying bitterly. Lynette said she was that child. It was in London during the war and her parents had just been killed in a bombing raid.

The man was one of her neighbours. He was desperately trying to take her to safety before more bombs fell. He first took her to an air-raid shelter, and later to an orphanage. But she was too young and confused to understand what was going on. She thought he'd kidnapped her from her happy home.

She only understood what had really happened a few years later. So it was a traumatic experience that had left her psyche wounded.

The neighbour who'd rescued her in the war was now her husband in this life. One of the reasons they were together was to heal this trauma. When people share dramatic experiences like this it can create a strong bond between them – especially if it needs to be healed in some way.

As Lynette talked this whole matter through after the regression, I could see the tension visibly leaving her. The strain in her face softened, and she looked years younger.

By the time she left, she was sure that she could make a new and happy future for herself and her husband. Knowing the past-life cause for her problem had made it easy to release it from her life.

Groups that reincarnate together

As well as our personal relationships, we can also have strong past-life ties to groups of people. If you were deeply involved with a particular set of people in a past life you may find them playing a similar role in your life again today.

For example, a weekly dream group may have been gathering for centuries to discuss spiritual matters. A football team that plays well together now may once have been sailors on the same ship. A choir may specialize in medieval music because that period was when they began singing together.

Belonging to a group from a past life can be a great source of emotional support. That's especially true if they are united around a deeply felt purpose. How they express that purpose will, of course, change according to the times. But if the sense of purpose remains strong, it will continue to hold the group together for more than one lifetime.

Groups from ancient civilizations

Groups of people may reincarnate from ancient civilizations. Sometimes they return on a mission to restore the lost wisdom of those worlds. In Chapter 6, Frances described how she wanted to bring the enlightened ways of ancient Minoa back into the world (*see page 71*).

Not knowing quite how to do that, she recently came for a second regression. During this session it became clear that she was not meant to shoulder this alone.

There were other ancient Minoans on Earth who shared this purpose. They were all part of the same team, and would recognize each other when they met. Her next step was to seek them out. Frances shed a tear of happy relief at this realization.

Return of the priestesses

At the beginning of the twentieth century, the mystic George Pickingill had an important message from his contacts on the inner planes. They said that a large and powerful group of priestesses from ancient Greece would soon be incarnating in the Western world. Their purpose would be to start laying the foundation for goddesses to become as honoured as the gods again.

Pickingill's role was to prepare the way for them. He began by changing traditional magic rituals to incorporate the male and female side in more equal ways. The long-term purpose of this huge project was to create a happier world based on a healthy balance of both yin and yang values.

Although there's still some way to go, the world has travelled far along that road since Pickingill's time. That may be at least partly thanks to the Grecian priestesses who decided to reincarnate as a group to serve this special purpose.

The Atlanteans

Edgar Cayce said that in the second half of the twentieth century a large group of Atlanteans would reincarnate in America. Their first purpose would be to create more social equality. Their second would be to bring back Atlantean technology to promote a more spiritually centred world.

In Cayce's time, before the middle of the twentieth century, inequality was an unquestioned way of life. And compared to now, technology wasn't in its infancy – it was barely out of the pram.

Since then, racism and sexism have become unacceptable, if not completely taboo. Technology has created a world that was undreamt of even 50 years ago. It looks like Edgar Cayce's prediction about the reincarnating group of Atlanteans has come true.

Soul groups from higher realms

My impression is that many other groups, both large and small, have also been reincarnating to follow a shared purpose. A number of my clients intuitively feel that they belong to a soul group.

Keith came for a regression because he wanted to discover his true identity. He accessed several lives in which he'd played the part of advisor to people in high places. His spirit guide told him that he is part of a soul group called the 'Shoulder Standers'. These are the people who, sometimes metaphorically and sometimes literally, stand at the shoulders of leaders.

They are there to try and nudge them towards the best paths and highest solutions that are available to them. Keith realized that membership of this group was both his mission and his true identity.

The University of Sirius

During a regression, Lucy recalled that at night she went in spirit to a kind of university in the constellation of Sirius. Evolved beings from there taught her and many others higher knowledge for them to bring back to Earth.

Lucy said going there felt like home. It was always a joyful experience. Among her fellow students, she recognized a few people from her everyday life here.

I asked if this university is for people who originally came from Sirius.

'Yes,' she said. 'It's for people who have always come from there and perhaps didn't know they did. But it's also for new people who are going in that direction – who are taking that path.'

A soul group is like a family. They may not always know why consciously, but they recognize, support and help one another because of this link. Although members of a soul group may be scattered across the world, they will regularly meet during dreamtime or in meditation.

How can you find out if you belong to a soul group? If you put out a wish to know more, information about it will start coming towards you. Messages and images may pop up in meditation. You could have vivid dreams about it. You might recognize some of the others from your group. As you put all this information together, the greater reality that you live in will become clearer.

Exercise: Meeting someone from a past life in the maze

A maze is like a puzzle that you have to walk through. The aim is to get to the centre. It's a challenge because the pathways are tricky. They're full of dead ends and wrong turnings. The paths are also lined with tall hedges that you can't see through or over.

During this exercise you'll meet someone in the maze who you know from a past life or a soul group. The following steps will help you to find out more about your relationship with them. You don't need to do all these steps every time – choose only those that feel appropriate.

Pick a time when you'll be quiet and undisturbed. Go through your favourite methods of relaxation.

1. Imagine that you're standing at the entrance to a maze. Walk in to the maze. Take whatever pathways feel right.

2. Soon you will meet someone in there. Notice every detail about their appearance. Do you recognize them in any way? What is their attitude towards you?

3. Ask if they have a message for you. They may talk to you, or show you something – perhaps a book or a picture.

4. Ask if you can do anything to help. They may ask for healing or forgiveness.

5. Ask if they can show you to the centre of the maze.

6. Exchange gifts with each other. These gifts are important symbols of your relationship and what it has brought to both of you.

When you feel ready to come out of this exercise, bid your companion goodbye until next time. Then simply open your eyes.

You can return to the maze whenever you wish to find out more about your relationships. As you do, it will give you all kinds of clues about past-life people in your life now, soul groups that you belong to, and the many pathways that you've all walked together.

***

SUMMARY

- Our relationships are full of past-life connections and clues. Becoming aware of that strengthens alliances, resolves issues, and adds a whole new dimension to our experience.

- Love and friendship are stronger than time. They can step over the centuries to find us. When we meet those people again, it feels like reuniting with an old friend from long ago.

- Pacts have the power to transcend lifetimes. They can call allies from the distant past back into our lives at just the right moment. Even if they cross our paths only briefly, those people can play a key role in our lives.

- Others may be with us because of unfinished past-life business that needs completion. To stop the issue dragging on lifetime after lifetime, the best course is usually to make peace in some way. This is possible even if the other person won't change. If you make your own positive changes with peace in your heart, it will finally free you from a weary situation.

- There are many kinds of past-life groups that we may belong to. Whether big or small, these groups can be a great source of inner support, comfort and inspiration. Knowing that we belong to a soul group transforms how we see ourselves, and adds a meaningful dimension to our lives.

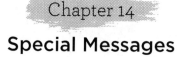

Chapter 14

Special Messages

A past-life memory will sometimes come up because it has a special, positive message for us. These messages come to give us hope when we're feeling down, confidence when we're feeling weak and a renewed sense of purpose when we're feeling lost.

Our inner self can find ways to get these messages through to us even without a regression. Dreams, meditation, intuitive feelings, signs and synchronicities are all good pathways that our spirits use to communicate with us.

Messages of hope

Sometimes our lives go through a dark patch. When that happens, it can be hard to see how or when it will end. At times like this, our past lives can be a great source of reassurance. They may show us that we've been through something similar before, and it turned out well in the end. They may also reconnect us with aspects of ourselves that will help us through the tough times.

Our lives often retrace the patterns of past-life experiences. But every time we repeat the pattern, it becomes easier and lighter. Once we've understood the underlying purpose of the experience, the lesson is done. That pattern will then fade away altogether.

Bombed out

In Bethany's regression, she went back to the Second World War. Her town had just been badly bombed. She said it felt like somewhere in Europe – perhaps Germany.

A bomb had smashed her home into a pile of rubble. She was frantically scrabbling through it, looking for her four children. With great relief, she eventually found them all frightened but safe in the cellar.

Then she had to figure out what to do next. They'd lost everything they owned. All they had was each other, and the clothes they were wearing. Her husband had recently been killed in battle, so she had only herself to rely on. She couldn't find any of her friends. They must have died in the raid. Her neighbours were cold towards her because she was foreign.

She decided to join the crowds who were walking to a refugee centre in the next town. It was a long way, especially for the children. Because she was different, none of the other people gave her any help along the way. But the little family got there in the end. They found a shelter that gave them hot soup and beds. From there, one small step at a time, the woman slowly rebuilt her life.

Some years later she remarried. She ended up living in a beautiful large house, cocooned in the warmth of friends and family again.

Bethany's spirit guide said that the memory had come up to show her that her current worries would have a similar happy ending.

This session took place during the dark days of the credit crunch. Bethany told me that she'd been badly affected by it. She didn't know how she'd ever recover. But she said this regression gave her reason to hope again. It felt like a major turning point. She knew that from now on life would start to get better.

Trust in life

Colleen came for a regression because of her asthma problems. Those issues were addressed during her regression, as described in Chapter 11 (see page 146). During the regression, she also accessed a memory that had an important message for her.

She went back to a life in Elizabethan England. She was an orphaned boy who lived on the streets. With his gang of fellow urchins, he spent his days begging or stealing food. At night they huddled together in cold doorways. But despite everything, he was cheerful and uncomplaining.

In his early teens, someone he'd begged from spotted his quick mind. They decided to take him up and train him as a servant. Thanks to that training, he later became a stable groom for an earl. He loved that job.

(Colleen later said she still loves horses. Her father was a country vet, and she grew up with them.)

Then one day disaster struck: the earl died. Along with most of the other servants, the stable groom was put out of work. He had to take a live-in job at an inn.

That place turned out to be the nerve centre for underground dealings and nefarious networks. It was an eye-opening experience and an education of sorts, but never as enjoyable as looking after the earl's horses had been.

The memory then jumped to the last phase of that life. He was living with his daughter and her family by then. Sitting in the garden, watching his grandchildren play, he was supremely contented.

He'd begun life with nothing, but had been blessed with good fortune. When it was time to pass on, he left that life with peace and gratitude in his heart.

Colleen's guide was a Tibetan monk. He said that this particular memory had come to show her that if you keep a positive attitude and trust that life will look after you, all will turn out well.

Afterwards Colleen said that this advice was exactly what she'd needed to hear. She'd been worrying far too much lately. This reminder was all she'd needed to put her back onto a positive course again.

Messages of self-worth

Our innate sense of self-worth – or lack of it – is one of the most powerful influences on our lives. It radiates out from us to all other areas of our experience. Lacking it, we find unconscious ways to reject the many gifts that life has to offer us. But when we have it, we enjoy life more. It also gives us the resilience to weather any difficulties that may come our way.

Sometimes our natural sense of self-worth can become deflated. At those times, getting a positive past-life message is like putting new air in flat tyres. It restores our natural bounce, making it easy for us to move ahead again with renewed confidence.

From jeers to cheers

In a past life, when Eddie was a boy of 14, angry villagers drove him out of the area. He thought it was because he was different in some way. But all he could recall was the devastating feeling of being violently rejected by everyone.

Later on, when the hue and cry had died down, he crept home again. But the incident left its mark on his psyche.

The next thing he recalled about that life was when he'd grown up. He was making a speech in the village hall. It was about a new system he'd thought up to distribute food to the poor. His audience listened with frowns and folded arms. The idea died on its feet.

The memory then shifted to some years later. He was swimming in a river race against other communities in the area. Everyone from his village turned out to cheer him on from the bridge and the riverbanks.

When he won the race, they were exultant. They carried him home on their shoulders. That night they gave him a big party. For the rest of that life, he was able to bask in the warm feeling that he'd not only been accepted at last – he'd also become a local hero.

Eddie's spirit guide told him that this memory had come up to reconnect him to that positive feeling, and to remind him that he could achieve whatever he set his mind to.

After the session, Eddie told me that a recent experience had knocked his confidence right down. He said that this memory, and the message it carried, had given him exactly what he needed to pick himself up again.

The capable monk

In his regression Gerry went back to a life as a senior monk in a Buddhist monastery. It was in a coastal town in the Far East.

One day a big storm came up. An old-style sailing ship crashed on the rocks. Gerry found himself directing the entire rescue operation.

The sailors from the ship were Chinese, so the local people were afraid of them. But with his influence as a senior monk, Gerry managed to reassure them. Before long, the people rallied round and helped to run a rescue centre for the distressed sailors.

The captain of the ship gave Gerry his heartfelt thanks for all that he'd done. After that, the memory faded.

Gerry's guide said this memory had come up to remind him of his hidden capabilities. This was partly to give his confidence a much-needed boost. It was also to let him know that he will help many people in this life as well.

Messages of purpose

Our past lives can also send us messages about the purpose of our soul journey – why we came here and what we really want to do with our lives.

This kind of reminder can have a transformative effect. Life begins to make sense again. We start seeing our experiences from a new, higher viewpoint. And we know more clearly what choices to make to create the future that was always meant to be our destiny.

The ancient initiate

Liana booked a holiday in Glastonbury because she had a strong feeling that it would do her good in some way.

As soon as she arrived, she kept noticing the word 'Thoth', and seeing pictures of him. Thoth was the ancient Egyptian god of communication. He's often shown holding a quill pen. The Greeks later called him Hermes, and for the Romans he was Mercury.

It seemed to Liana that something to do with Thoth was trying to get through to her. Her lodgings had a beautiful jacuzzi that she could use and as it was a quiet time, she could have it to herself. She decided to use it to relax and allow messages from her inner self to surface.

With an aromatherapy burner scenting the air, she sank into the warm bubbles. The tub was surrounded by large house plants. The candles she'd lit created softly moving shadows around her. She drifted into deep relaxation.

'Then suddenly, in my mind's eye, I saw Thoth,' she said. 'It was as if he was standing in front of me. He was looking straight at me. He said "My initiates are waking up now." Then the image faded.

'I was a bit startled by that. I was beginning to feel chilly, so I got out and went up to my room. I lay on my bed and fell asleep – and had an amazing dream.

'I saw Thoth initiating and training many people – including myself. That began in ancient Egypt. But it's been continuing on the inner planes ever since. It's been going on during my life now. When I leave my body at night, that's where I go. I just wasn't ready to know about that till now.'

I asked what the teachings were about. Liana said it was to do with spiritual communications, and how to transmit them. She said she'd always had ambitions to be a writer, but hadn't made much progress yet.

'I think now that may be because I had the wrong focus,' she mused. 'My heart wasn't in the kind of writing I thought I had to do. But I know now that I should write about what feels right for me.'

It's my impression that many people belong to higher-dimensional groups that are also part of their past-life history. These groups are usually to do with your work, your spiritual path or a special purpose. When you're ready to know more, information about it will start to come to you.

Special messages about our soul journey can be important turning points in our lives. They open up the way to a new future by reminding us of how life once was for us – and how it could be again.

SUMMARY

Your inner spirit can speak to you in many ways. Messages may come to you through intuition, dreams, signs, synchronicities, hunches, meditation, inner feelings or regression. When the time is right, messages will come to:

- Wake up qualities and abilities that will help you through life now.

- Help you over a rough patch by reminding you of how you overcame adversity before.

- Restore your confidence and sense of self-worth.

- Show you which past-life and soul groups you belong to.

- Reveal your life purpose.

When we know how to listen to them, all our past lives have special messages for us. They buoy us up with reminders of our joys, triumphs and achievements. They explain our problems and help us to solve them. And they enrich all our experiences with a deeper view of ourselves, the way of the world, and the meaning of life itself.

Chapter 15

Where Next for You?

What about your own past lives? If you feel drawn to the subject, it's a sign that you're ready to find out more.

The best way to set anything off is to make a decision about it. Decisions are powerful tools – they get things moving. If you're curious about your past lives, simply decide that it's time to discover more about them.

Hypnotherapist Arnall Bloxham said, 'Just ask "who am I, the eternal me, who has lived before?" and that will start you remembering past lives.'

An intriguing adventure of discovery will then unfold. Past-life memories will start coming to you in all kinds of ways.

Possible pathways to the past

For example, you may suddenly realize that a favourite picture on your wall shows life in a time or place that you've always felt attracted to. You wonder if you might have once lived there. Clues and synchronicities could then come up to confirm that you did.

Or you might discover that something you were good at in childhood was a past-life ability. A vivid dream set in old times may show you when you first learned that skill.

You may feel drawn to attend a past-life workshop. Perhaps one of their guided visualizations gives you a useful overview of your soul journey. This seems to point to developing your past-life skill in this life. When you look it up, your astrology chart may back this up.

Curious for more details, you try dowsing with a pendulum to get more specific answers. Wanting to confirm that information in another way, your next step might be a meditation exercise or a regression.

This is just one example of the many different pathways that can open up for you as you explore your past lives.

Let your heart lead the way. If something feels like a good idea, follow it up. If it doesn't, this may not be the right time for it. As you go along, little by little, you'll build up a good picture of your past lives and their relevance to you now.

Key questions

When past-life memories come up, you can get the best from them by asking the following questions. You can put these questions to the universe, your inner self, higher consciousness, angels or spirit guides – whichever feels right for you.

The answers will then come to you through dreams, synchronicities, sudden realizations, meditation, visualization or regression. The way it works for me is simply to put a question to my inner self – the deeper levels of consciousness within the psyche. When I wake up the next morning, the answer downloads into my mind. Big questions may take a bit longer, but an answer always comes in the end.

These questions are a foundation and a starting point. As other questions occur to you, continue using your favourite methods to find out more.

1. How did that life affect me?

2. What beliefs or attitudes did I adopt because of that life?

3. Do those beliefs now help or hinder me?

4. What special thing did I learn in that life?

5. How can that benefit me now?

6. Is there any unfinished business left over from that life?

7. How can I complete that?

8. What is the special gift to me from that life?

It's best to deal with these questions one at a time. Move on to the next question when you've had an answer to the first one you asked. Make a note of the answers you receive, whatever way they may come to you. Sometimes the universe can send us answers in the next e-mail or article we read. Even an overheard comment from a passing stranger can be a magical message to us.

It's helpful to ask these questions because the great benefit of discovering past lives is understanding how they still affect you. This releases you from their negative effects. It also reconnects you with all that was good about them. In these ways, our past lives have the power to transform our present life and create a positive new future for us.

The round table

Remembering past lives also gives us an expanded view of the greater soul self. It shows us that we are so much more than just one person. This awareness frees us from many fears that belong only to the little self. It shows us a joyfully higher view of the world, our lives and ourselves.

For most of us, this new horizon has only just begun to open up. It's exciting, but can also be a bit confusing. It will be easier to integrate if you can see it as a symbolic image – for example, a round table.

The circle stands for wholeness. Tables represent how people gather together. The round table therefore has archetypal significance as an emblem of harmony and equality. Seeing your past and future selves at your round table will help to make this new expanded consciousness more real for you.

Go through the usual preparations that you do before any meditation or inner work. Then imagine your round table in a beautiful place – for example in a garden, a woodland clearing or a twilit beach.

Every time you discover who you were in a new past life, bring them to the table and make them welcome. This will do much to heal old problems from that life. It will also strengthen the positive effects of that life on you now.

You can visit your round table whenever you wish. Not only to bring new people to it, but just to see if everyone's happy, and if anyone new has dropped in.

The giant jigsaw

The different pieces of your past-life history are like a huge jigsaw. As you put them together, a bigger picture will come into view. That picture will not only show you the many different lives you've had – it will also make it clear that your current self and life are part of a much greater context.

As you explore your past lives you'll discover your spiritual identity and the long-term purpose of your soul journey here on Earth.

You'll find from deep within yourself the answers to the age-old questions: Who am I? Where did I come from? And why am I here?

Bibliography

Andrews, Ted. *How to Uncover Your Past Lives*, Llewellyn, 2006

Barker, Jennifer and Roger Woolger. *The Goddess Within,* Rider, 1990

Bernstein, Morey. *The Search for Bridey Murphy*, Random House, 2002

Bowman, Carol. *Children's Past Lives*, Thorsons, 1998

Browne-Miller, Angela. *Embracing Death*, Bear & Co., 1996

Carpenter, Sue. *Past Lives*, Virgin Books, 1995

Cayce, Edgar Evans. *Edgar Cayce on Atlantis*, Little, Brown & Company, 2000

Cayce, Hugh. *Edgar Cayce on Dreams*, Warner Books, 1995

Cerminara, Gina. *Many Mansions*, Penguin Books, 1993

Cockell, Jenny. *Yesterday's Children*, Piatkus, 1993

Danelik, J. Allan. *The Mystery of Reincarnation*, Authors' Choice Press, 2007

Fisher, Joe. *The Case for Reincarnation*, Somerville House Books, 1998

Fisher, Joe. *Coming Back Alive*, Souvenir Press Ltd, 2001

Fortune, Dion. *Dion Fortune's Book of the Dead*, Red Wheel/ Weiser, 2005

Goldberg, Bruce. *New Age Hypnosis*, Llewellyn, 1998

Goldberg, Bruce. *Past Lives, Future Lives*, Ballantine, 1993

Guirdham, Arthur. *The Cathars and Reincarnation*, C.W. Daniel Co. Ltd, 1990

Guirdham, Arthur. *A Foot in Both Worlds*, C.W. Daniel Co. Ltd., 1992

Guirdham, Arthur. *The Lake and the Castle*, C.W. Daniel Co. Ltd., 1991

Head, J., and S.L. Cranston. *Reincarnation in World Thought*, Theosophical Publishing House, 1970

Ingerman, Sandra. *Soul Retrieval*, HarperOne, 2010

Iverson, Jeffrey. *More Lives Than One?* Macmillan, 1977

Jung, Carl. *Memories, Dreams, Reflections*, Fontana, 1995

Jung, Carl. *Modern Man in Search of a Soul*, Routledge, 2001

Jussek, Eugene G. *Reaching for the Oversoul*, Hays (Nicolas) Ltd, 1994

Knight, Gareth. *Dion Fortune and the Inner Light*, Thoth Publications, 2000

Kubler-Ross, Elisabeth, and Raymond Moody, *Life After Life*, Rider, 2001

Langs, Robert. *Decoding Your Dreams*, Ballantine, 1990

Lin, Denise. *Past Lives, Present Dreams*, Piatkus, 1994

Mindel, Arnold. *Dreambody*, Deep Democracy Exchange, 2011

Mindel, Arnold. *Working with the Dreaming Body*, Lao Tse Press, 2001

Moody, Raymond. *Glimpses of Eternity*, Rider, 2011

Moody, Raymond. *Life Before Life*, Pan, 1991

Moss, Robert. *Conscious Dreaming*, Rider, 2013

Newton, Michael. *Destiny of Souls*, Llewellyn, 2000

Newton, Michael. *Journey of Souls*, Llewellyn, 1994

Newton, Michael. *Life Between Lives*, Llewellyn, 2004

Parnia, Sam. *What Happens When We Die*, Hay House, 2008

Rossetti, Francesca. *Psycho Regression*, Red Wheel/Weiser, 1994

Sachs, Robert. *Perfect Endings*, Healing Arts Press, 1998

Stemman, Roy. *Reincarnation*, Piatkus, 2004

Stevenson, Ian. *20 Cases Suggestive of Reincarnation*, University of Virginia Press, 1988

Wambach, Helen. *Life Before Life*, Bantam, 1981

Wambach, Helen. *Reliving Past Lives*, Barnes & Noble, 1984

Weiss, Brian. *Many Lives, Many Masters*, Piatkus, 1994

Weiss, Brian. *Messages from the Masters*, Piatkus, 2000

Weiss, Brian. *Same Soul, Many Bodies*, Piatkus, 2004

Woolger, Roger. *Healing Your Past Lives*, Sounds True Inc., 2010

Woolger, Roger. *Other Lives, Other Selves*, Thorsons, 1999

Index

ABOUT THE AUTHOR

Atasha Fyfe graduated with a BA (Hons) degree, taught high-school history and English and then entered the world of journalism. She knew in her heart, however, that these experiences were in many ways a preparation for her true calling.

Her deepest interest was spiritually centred psychology, and to develop this she studied widely and took courses in Rogerian Counselling, Hypnotherapy and Transpersonal Psychology. She then felt inspired to move from London to Glastonbury, where she discovered that her clients were primarily interested in finding out about their past lives.

Realizing this was life's special gift to her, Atasha embraced the subject wholeheartedly. An experienced shaman gave her private tuition in past-life regression, and she researched everything she could on the subject. At the same time, she regularly began to publish articles in New Age and esoteric magazines.

A fascinating journey unfolded, during which she built up a large data bank of case studies and made many exciting discoveries about the greater awareness and potentials that are available to us all.

If you'd like to share your own past-life experiences and insights, you're welcome to contact Atasha through her website.

www.pastlivesglastonbury.co.uk

HAY HOUSE

Look within

Join the conversation about latest products,
events, exclusive offers and more.

 Hay House UK

 @HayHouseUK

@hayhouseuk

healyourlife.com

We'd love to hear from you!

Printed in the United States
by Baker & Taylor Publisher Services